My Winnipeg

Guy Maddin

Coach House Books

first edition

The film *My Winnipeg* deliberately blurs the line between fact and fiction. No attempt has been made to distinguish the two, and so there may be significant factual errors in the script, narration and essays. Please don't read this book as historical truth.

Every effort has been made to contact copyright holders of images and text; please notify Coach House Books if we've made an error or omission and we will correct it in subsequent editions.

 Canada Council   Conseil des Arts    ONTARIO ARTS COUNCIL   Canadä
for the Arts   du Canada   CONSEIL DES ARTS DE L'ONTARIO

Published with the generous assistance of the Canada Council for the Arts and the Ontario Arts Council. Coach House Books also acknowledges the support of the Government of Ontario through the Ontario Book Publishing Tax Credit and the Government of Canada through the Book Publishing Industry Development Program.

LIBRARY AND ARCHIVES CANADA CATALOGUING IN PUBLICATION (WITH DVD)

Maddin, Guy
    My Winnipeg / Guy Maddin.

Script of the film, My Winnipeg, with annotations, accompanied by a DVD.
    Book also issued seperately.
ISBN 978-1-55245-212-7

    1. My Winnipeg (Motion picture). 2. Maddin, Guy. 3. Winnipeg (Man.)--
Miscellanea. 4. Motion picture producers and directors--Manitoba--Winnipeg--
Biography. I. Title.

PN1997.2.M92 2009a   791.43'72   C2009-902193-5

LIBRARY AND ARCHIVES CANADA CATALOGUING IN PUBLICATION (WITHOUT DVD)

Maddin, Guy
    My Winnipeg / Guy Maddin.

Script of the film, My Winnipeg, with annotations. Book also issued accompanied
    by a DVD.
ISBN 978-1-55245-211-0

    1. My Winnipeg (Motion picture). 2. Maddin, Guy. 3. Winnipeg (Man.)--
Miscellanea. 4. Motion picture producers and directors--Manitoba--Winnipeg--
Biography. I. Title.

PN1997.2.M92 2009   791.43'72   C2009-901774-1

Table of Contents

My Winnipeg   7

{An annotated script by Guy Maddin,
replete with photographs, collages, animations
and other *My Winnipeg* arcana}

Guy Maddin and Michael Ondaatje:
A Conversation   129

{Conducted at the Cobourg
in Toronto, November 2008}

A Miscellany   153

{A treasure trove,
including colour photographs and art,
notebook excerpts, and reflections
by Andy Smetanka, Darcy Fehr and Caelum Vatnsdal}

The End   190

{Filmography, image credits, acknowledgements}

Remove all emotional coloring

SHOT—LIST   CUTS
THE INTRO   what's on VIDEO, R.S., BOLEX

Winnipeg
OUTLINE/SCRIPT
20th February 2006

NIGHTSPOT VIDEO on sleepwalkers @ night

Give the film a unified look – including limited palette, limited locations: the alleys, the snow, coziness, old, dark, palimpsesty, peeling, railways and fog, frosty, ENCHANTED SOMEHOW! Limit the geography. Keep the film thematically focused! Or else Winnipeg will simply look like every other North American Mid-western city!!!!

STORYBOARD FRIEZE ARTICLE!

Intro

= Get a Repair: What kind of city is this? Does this? Has it

Back Lanes, Sleepwalkers & Heartsick Architecture

OPENING SHOT: **"Love Me, Love My Winnipeg"** sign at the Bridge Drive In. Or: **The Blank Billboards** at the city limits?
Propel the film into its arc: I NEED TO LEAVE THIS CITY!

-French fur trader spelling of Winnipeg: Ouinipique!

The film starts with a brisk narrated introduction to my home town and my discomfort with it, my perceived need to leave it once and for all.

Discussed by way of illustrating what has benumbed me with an unpleasant enchantment, and what powers currently enchant this town:

-A brief look at the town's location and history, including the conditions which Sir Arthur Conan Doyle described as most conducive to psychic phenomenon (The First Nations belief in the powers of the river forks both above and deeply below the earth's surface – these forks being the meeting place of animal and hunter trails above, and of spirit pathways below; the city's continental centeredness; its nearness to the influences of the aurora borealis; the strange IMMEMORIAL migratory powers of the bison; the endless unseen coupling and uncoupling of **trains** whose steel lines gird and bind our continent like so much string on a package of meat!)

Tighten up # of cast members

From Guy Maddin's My Winnipeg *notebook*

My Winnipeg

{An annotated script by Guy Maddin,
replete with photographs, collages, animations and other *My Winnipeg* arcana}

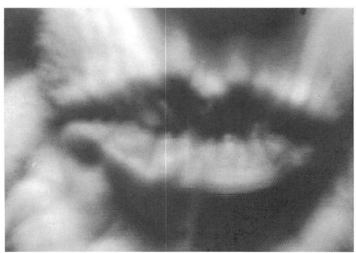 

Grace Hospital, Winnipeg, Man. Canada

I was born on the 28th of February, 1956, at old Grace Hospital, corner of Arlington and Preston, just as Canada's first candystripers were introduced there – surely a salutary omen. (Legendary teen Hollywood movie star Deanna Durbin was born in the same ward in 1921.) Fifty years later, after the end of a long relationship with a girlfriend, I found myself crashing at my friend Robert Enright's apartment, right across the street from the old Grace. Nice to know that in half a century, much of that time spent planning my escape from Winnipeg, I'd ended up precisely 100 feet from my birthplace.

My Winnipeg

Guy Maddin

All aboard!

Winnipeg.
Winnipeg.
Winnipeg.
Snowy, sleepwalking Winnipeg.

My home for my entire life.
My entire life.

I must leave it.
I must leave it.
I must leave it now.

But how to escape one's city?
How to wake oneself enough for
the frightening task?
And how to find one's way out?

The greatest urban train yard in the world.
Arteries! Iron veins! Ways out!!!
The dream train!
Chugging, dreaming, sleep-chugging,
out of the lap of the city.

Out of the lap described by the Forks:
of the Red, the Assiniboine.

The name *Winnipeg* is a transcription of a Western Cree word meaning *murky waters.*

Winnipeg was originally spelled *Ouinipique* by Sieur de La Vérendrye, the French officer who built the first fur-trading post on the site in 1738.

A resident of Winnipeg is a *Winnipegger,* or *'Pegger.* Significantly, *peggered,* the Winnipeg bastardization of the Yiddish past participle *gepeygert,* which means *dropped dead,* suggests, by working backwards to the infinitive, that *to pegger* means *to die.* I am certainly not a Yiddish scholar, but this word is generally well accepted and utilized here, with much morbid glee and civic self-awareness.

Winnipeg – like Columbus, Ohio, long one of those guinea pig–packed cities where product innovations are test-marketed – became, in 1959, the first city in the world to amalgamate emergency phone numbers into the 911 all North Americans use today. To make matters worse, just a few years later we became the first city to use Touch-Tone phones. (Available in the CBC television archives is a December 8, 1959, broadcast of the local show *Eye to Eye* that visits our 999 emergency switchboard, talking with the people who run the service and hearing some of the calls – including one from a girl whose sister has swallowed a marble: http://archives.cbc.ca/science_technology/technology/clips/6261/

It was my good friend Noam Gonick – Winnipeg's notorious Night Mayor, or Nightmare, also known by the Wilhelm Reichian moniker 'that Jewish pornographer of the most dangerous sort' – who told me of this deeply moving Aboriginal legend while helping me walk Spanky. Over the years he has during such strolls filled my head practically to bursting with Winnipeg dazzlements, many of which I have wafted into my movies.

Like all of us Winnipeggers, Noam has had his own first-hand experience with the wintry waters and mystical transformative powers of the Forks. As a fourth-grader, he invented the now-popular Winnipeg sight gag of kneeling in the deep snow that lies upon the frozen river crust, flailing his arms as if he'd just broken through to water and crying out for help.

One day he wandered too close to an openly flowing sewer outlet at the edge of the river. (Perhaps the sweetly perfumed bathwaters and fecal deposits of wealthy Tuxedo-area residents were luring him, he who was already a child of Bolshevik tendencies, to a shortened and therefore less dangerously effective life as the Winnipeg middle class's subversive enemy?) Suddenly, the ice beneath his feet opened into a chasm, collapsing the boy into the fetid stream. He was treading water but, garbed in a thick, sponge-like snowsuit, he knew it was a matter of seconds before he was sunk and lost.

Initially, his mates thought he was still playing his short-legged game, but eventually they came to his rescue. A friend's older cousin, an all-around athletic star who was in Grade 7, knew exactly how to lie splayed across the ice while pulling little Noamie out, a trick all Winnipeg children learn but pray they'll never have to use.

Noam, with the help of his lithe rescuer, scampered up the riverbank, his winterwear freezing into a rigid girdle, to his friend's house, where he was hauled through a housewives' sherry party and into the bathroom. There, the athletic cousin took charge of operations: steam filled the washroom as Boy Noamie was summarily stripped and plunged under a hot shower to thaw the hypothermia. With alacrity, the resourceful boy-athlete-cum-nurse laid out the floor towels for the now-naked little shiverer, all the better for a good daub at his *eisschweiss*. Noam, the soaked pup, was instructed by his new hero to lie down, and was given a vigorous body massage that focused manfully on his still-chilled nether regions. The friend's more experienced cousin had saved Noam's young life but, in that moment, this suave and strapping youth also gave Noam a brand-new life, indefatigably warming the lad till somewhere a little flame ignited. And to this day, Winnipeg's Nightmare, now grown to fecund adulthood, thanks to the spirit of the city, still gives his blessings to the gods of lust and ice water for his life, and this life's life – his Desire. It is the way of the Forks.

The forks:
Assiniboine and the Red.
The rivers that forced animals and hunters alike
onto the same waterside pathways.

The forks, the lap.
The forks, the lap.
The forks, the lap.

The reason we are here, right here,
in the centre of the continent.
The heart of the heart of the continent.

The hunted lap.
The woolly lap.
The lap of my mother.

Arteries. The forks beneath the Forks:
an old tale from the First Nations has it
that there are subterranean forks,
two secret rivers meeting,
directly beneath the Assiniboine and Red,
this double pairing of rivers being
extra supernaturally powerful.
The animals, the hunters,
the boatways, water and rails.
These are the reasons we are here.

Pulling out of the station.
Pulling out of the station.

The 'Heart of the Continent' is what local fifties TV weatherman Ed Russenholt used to call Winnipeg. He would draw a big black grease-pencil heart around a Plexiglas map of our frigid environs at the end of each ghostly broadcast, then let out a soul-weary sigh. Many people have asked if, with this juiced-up version of Russenholt's shibboleth, I was paying tribute to William Gass's short-story masterpiece 'In the Heart of the Heart of the Country,' a tale set in the deeply hallucinatory cold of a snowbound prairie landscape identical to Manitoba's. I must say that I was not. But I'll accept this highly pedigreed accidental literary buttressing up of this, my humble travelogue.

The lap: I've often said the hardest part of shooting *My Winnipeg* was tugging the girdle off my mom for these nude shots of a female lap. But almost everyone believes these snug thighs belong to my ex-girlfriend, Erin Hershberg. I promised her I would set the record straight in these notes: I do hereby swear that the naked lap in *My Winnipeg* does not belong to Erin Hershberg!

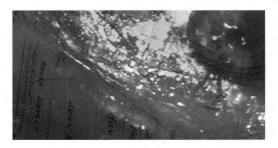

Preparatory collage by Carl Matheson

1914. Two great events happen without Winnipeggers really noticing much, though these events will determine forever the quality of life here for me and my fellow citizens. They occur almost simultaneously.

First, the ribbon is cut to open the Panama Canal, the beginning of the end for Winnipeg as a major hub for all transcontinental shipping by rail. The result? The city's downtown, booming for decades, suddenly stops growing, suspends itself, as if in amber. No new buildings have been erected in our central Exchange District since the slicing of that ribbon!

Then, a second laceration – that of my father's eye. Clutching her infant son to her bosom on his first birthday, my grandmother pierces his eye with a carelessly unpinned brooch. Doctors are unable to save it. It is removed and buried with the rest of the city's medical waste – its amputated limbs and its dissected med-school cadavers – in a mass grave at Brookside Cemetery. It is sixteen years before my father's family can afford to buy him his first glass eye.

The doctors try to relieve my grandmother's guilt by telling her they discovered a tumour in the little one's eye socket and, had it not been removed at this opportune time, his life would certainly have been claimed by this rampaging infantile cancer. She doesn't believe the doctors, choosing instead to dedicate her life to removing eyes. She spends the rest of her days poking the eyes out of her own likeness in photos – never forgetting the role she played in scooping out a little hollow in that baby's head. Never forgetting. Now there isn't a single photo of my grandmother without her eyes poked out.

Strange is the role of memory in this city that no longer recollects why it's even here. Even stranger is the way the city buries its amnesias in further layers of forgetfulness.

What if I had already left decades ago?
What if? What if?
Winnipeg.

Always winter.
Always winter.
Always sleeping.
Winnipeg. Winnipeg. Winnipeg.

The train tracks cross the streetcar tracks
and in turn cross the streets and the alleyways,
everything beneath thin layers
of time, asphalt and snow.
Are these arteries still here today?
Are they dug out every night
and reconcealed every dawn?
We Winnipeggers are so stupefied with
nostalgia we're actually never quite sure.
I never really know anything for sure –
except that after a lifetime of trying
and many botched attempts,
this time I'm leaving for good.
Again.

Back in Winnipeg's earliest years,
the Canadian Pacific Railway
used to sponsor an annual treasure hunt.
This contest required our citizens
to wander the city in a day-long combing
of our streets and neighbourhoods.

Darcy Fehr, who sits in for me in the train-carriage sequences, was thirty-two years old at the time of production, precisely the age at which I should have left town for good.

I stumbled upon this perhaps too frequently used rhetorical device of repetition in triplets when I accidentally hypnotized, or at least sent off to sleep, my recording engineer Michel Germain while improvising narration for *My Winnipeg* in the studio. As was my practice whenever I stepped behind a microphone in those days, I attempted to riff on Winnipeg in one continuous flow, without ever stopping – not even once – and whenever I ran out of facts, laments or historical accounts I would simply keep repeating the last phrase spoken just to keep the clock running until I dreamed up something new to say. Excited by the coma of my studio compadre, who was slumped face-first onto the buttoned panel of the recording console, I realized I possessed the power of a Mesmer, Reveen, Romane or any of the immortal stage hypnotists and their ilk, and that rather than squandering this eerie power pulling the bras off beautiful women – oh, the ephemeral vanity of that gesture! – I would use it in the service of cinema ... to hypnotize my entire audience. How naive I was in those earliest days of what has become a fearsome new era for me.

My mother was born with the very Icelandic name Jörina Herdis Eyolfson. (When spoken with the proper Icelandic singsong accent, her Christian names are pronounced *You're gonna hurt us.*) She came into being in Vestfold, Manitoba, on the 9th of November, 1916. I've always used the year of her birth as the PIN for my credit and debit cards, and *Herdis* has for years now been my trusty password for all my online purchases.

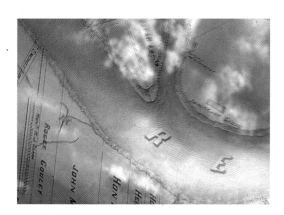

First prize was a one-way ticket
on the next train out of town.
The idea being that once someone had spent
a full day looking this closely at his own
hometown he would never want to leave.
That the real treasure was right here
all along.
And you know what?
Not one treasure-hunt winner ever
got on that train and left.
Not one, not in a hundred years.
Well, I don't need a treasure hunt.
I've got my own ticket.
I just have to make my way through town,
through everything I've ever seen and lived,
everything I've loved and forgotten.
Through the thick furry frost
and out to the city limits.
Then I'm on my way.
Out of here.
Out from the heart
of the heart of the continent.

The woolly, furry, frosty lap.
The Forks!
The animals, hunters, boatways,
trains and Mother.
These are the reasons we're here.
These are these reasons we've stayed.
These are the reasons I'm leaving.

This annual contest now traditionally starts at our war memorial, which rises out of the centre of what no one remembers was once called the Mall.

Emblematic of our city's curious ways of remembrance is the saga of this cenotaph, erected to honour our war dead. In the 1920s, there was a contest to determine who would design it, the only condition being that it must commemorate the lives lost in the Great War. After it was built, there was a public outcry when it was discovered that its designer, one Emanuel Hahn, was born in Germany, the very country responsible for snatching all those precious lives away. It was torn down and another contest was held. The winner this time was a Canadian-born sculptress, Elizabeth Wood, and after her cenotaph was built there was more outrage when it was discovered that this sculptress was in fact married to Emanuel Hahn. Finally, in typically cautious Canadian fashion, the designer who finished second to the sculptress was passed over and the third-place finisher, the very Anglo-Saxon-sounding Gilbert Parfitt, was given the commission to build the memorial that, to this day, stands as the lone official civic commemoration of Winnipeg's World War I dead.

These are the very things that are going to
help me get out of here.

The forks, the lap, the fur.
The forks, the lap, the fur.

Mother appears occasionally on the train
to check on the passengers.
My mother. A force as strong
as all the trains in Manitoba.
As perennial as the winter.
As ancient as the bison.
As supernatural as the Forks themselves.
Her lap, a magnetic pole,
a direction from which I can't turn for long.

It must be the sleepiness
that keeps Winnipeggers here.
If only I can stay awake,
pay attention to where I'm going, where I've been,
and get out of here.
Stay awake. Stay awake.
Stay awake, Winnipegger!

We sleep as we walk. Walk as we dream.
Winnipeg has ten times the sleepwalking
rate of any other city in the world.
And because we dream of where we walk
and walk to where we dream,
we are always lost, befuddled.

From Guy Maddin's My Winnipeg *notebook*

The E Gang! In the 1980s, Winnipeg trembled beneath the thumb of the E Gang, an elusive group of nocturnal criminals whose sole crime, repeated endlessly and always with impunity, for the identity of its members was never ascertained by the police, was stealing the letter E from every piece of signage in the city. Our city became even more elliptical that decade: The Winnip g Ar na; arl Gr y and Gr nway schools; aton's; Th Paddl wh l; The W vil Caf ; K-T l Int rna-tional; even Lil's B auty Shop. We realized this was a letter we could easily live without, that even in its absence it was really still there. One excit-ing night, perhaps because I expressed so much public support for these mischievous gangsters, I was blindfolded and taken to their lair to behold the booty of their long exertions. What I saw mounded there, or hung about the place as queer trophies, was nothing less than gorgeous. The letter E in every possible font, in all sizes, fash-ioned from every conceivable material – moulded plaster, carved wood, cursive driftwood, neon tubing, tin, cast iron, punched zinc and incan-descent clusters of glass! A garden of Eeeeden!

Rejected narration: Bedless shadows befuddled.

Guy Maddin, citizen of the afternoon

Winnipeggers are very forgetful, and often repeat themselves without realizing it – and not just the things they say. Often they entirely redo things, just to be sure. A certain amount of repetition has made its way into acceptable public behaviour in the city. Ritual repetitions help people achieve certainty in life – a handshake in greeting or a wave goodbye is never considered complete until it's been performed as many as twelve times. Winnipeggers meeting out in society are considered rude whenever they don't ask each other how they've been at least a half-dozen times. In this fashion we make of ourselves human palimpsests concealing one gesture or persona beneath its identical issue.

Asleep on foot,
the Winnipegger is a citizen of the night.
The Winnipeg night.
Why is this so?
Why are we so sleepy?
Why can't we just open our eyes?
Is it the mystically paired river forks,
the bio-magnetic influence of our bison?
The powerful northern lights?
We don't know.
We sleep.
We sleepwalk.
We sleepwalk.

We show up on old doorsteps …
old homes … our old homes …
those of our old sweethearts …
and we are allowed by civic law to carry
the keys of these old dreamy domiciles.
Of these old dreamy addresses.
And those who live at the old homes
must always take in a lost sleepwalker.
Must let the confused one stay till he wakes.
In Winnipeg, it's the law.

These old dreamy addresses, keys, keys.

Winnipeg.

Home.

Rejected narration: The Winnipegger, a man of great sleep, bedlessness himself, is a citizen of night.

Rejected narration: Berimed, slush-splashed and soiled with mourning; heavy-footed, heavy-legged, heavy-headed with the weight of leaden dreams, we show up on old doorsteps …

Rejected narration: And bedlessness seeks doors, doorknobs, keyholes!

In 2005, breakcore musician, Budapest resident and expat Winnipegger Aaron Funk, who records under the name Venetian Snares, released on Sublight Records *Winnipeg Is a Frozen Shithole*. Its track list:

1. Winnipeg Is a Frozen Shithole
2. Winnipeg Is a Dogshit Dildo
3. Winnipeg Is Fucking Over
4. Winnipeg Is Steven Stapleton's Armpit
5. Die Winnipeg Die Die Die Fuckers Die
6. Winnipeg as Mandatory Scat Feed
7. Winnie the Dog Pooh (Not Half Remix)
8. Winnipeg Is a Boiling Pot of Cranberries (Fanny Remix)
9. Die Winnipeg Die Die Die Fuckers Die (Spreading the Hepatitis SKM-ETR Style)

By the time I'm born, my grandmother is in her eighties and blind from the glaucoma that drops through our family's generations. She lives with us and, never forgetting, endlessly acts out, by rote, the few rituals to which, in her dark boredom, she has reduced herself – napping frequently, listening to the radio and singing old Icelandic work songs to herself in her rocker. Sometimes I'll creep silently in on her, holding my breath while she takes an hour to thread a needle, just to pass the time. Most intriguingly, she keeps up her lifelong project of pricking out all the photographed eyes of herself, even though she has years ago run out of such pictures to mutilate. She recruits my help; as her amanuensis, I write away to relatives for more portraits, and when they arrive in the mail I guide her hand over their daguerreotype surfaces to the spot where her girlish gaze sits in the ancient emulsions, then – *pop! pop!* – her needle pushes through the image and her eyes are gone once more in a tiny explosion of paper.

Eventually there are no more pictures of her, or at least no more living relatives who can send us any. Now we write to the dead relatives. My grandmother is blind so I can fake the correspondence – that is, I can write to myself. With my grandmother closely supervising by touch, I write and she signs each enquiring missive. But having no ungouged pictures of the tormented woman to mail back to us, I discreetly slide some spare snapshots of my own family into an envelope and post it right back to our own address, so that a week later I tear open the same envelope, produce for her the familial totems and help her remove, with her needle, what she thinks are her eyes but are in fact the eyes of my brothers, sister and mother – even Toby, our chihuahua. Deoculated, all!

Soon bored by this geriatric hobby, I go so far as to guide her fingers onto the photographic face of my father and let her again pierce his fatefully aggrieved eye.

Unlike other sleepwalkers who carry with
themselves great balls of keys,
keys to all their old addresses,
I keep just the one key with me at all times,
the key to 800 Ellice.

Home.
Dreams,
dreaming,
dreaming.

Every night I have the same happy dream
that I'm back in my old childhood home.
It was the biggest house in the
neighbourhood, also the strangest.
I was proud of this strangeness,
ashamed too, depending on
who saw me enter its front door,
for it was actually three structures in one.
Most embarrassingly, a beauty salon
run by my mom and my aunt Lil.
A sprawling seven-room suite in back
for my aunt and grandmother.
And up top, a big baby-boomer bedroom
cluster for my mom, dad,
three siblings Ross, Cam, Janet,
and Toby, our chihuahua,
our long, long, long-dead
chihuahua.

Dream Diary: Dreamt last night of my father,
lying sick and sad on his back in the bed he
shared with Mother. I entered the room from his
left and could see only his left eye, his glass eye,
staring ceilingward, so he could not see me. As
he has for the past thirty years, my father disappeared to the spot, still unknown to this day,
where he always hides from his family when he
dies, and I find myself the inheritor of my
parents' bedroom.

Strangely, Mother has now taken over my
bed.

Beyond my new parental couch, Mother's
bathroom is all frilly towels and curtains, floral
bath salts and oils – towels that are more flounce
than business. These are now to be my permanent quarters, while Mother, from this point
forward, is confined to my bedroom, forced to
use my aquarium for a chamber pot.

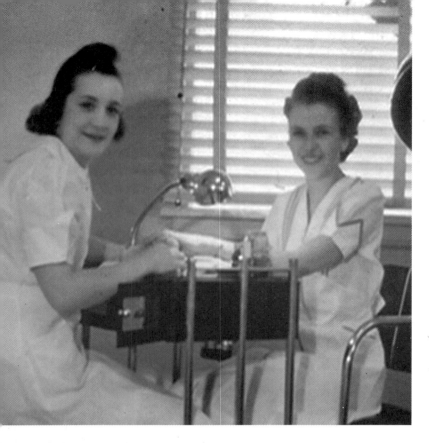

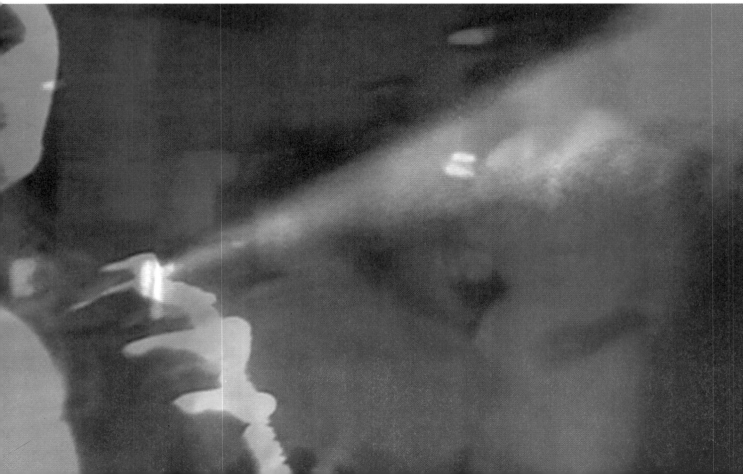

A big cube of home.
A chunk of happy home.
I've often wondered what effect
growing up in a hair salon had on me.
Designed by my mother in 1940.
I loved the noises.
The shop always a-whir with gossip!
Laughter! Buzzing! Snipping!
The clatter of trays dropped on the floor.
Door chimes, the phone always ringing.
Shrieks. Shrieks over the roar of the dryers!
The air always acrid with lotions,
or fuzzy with sprays –
cloudy, cloudy, cloudy with hairsprays.
Helmets! Helmets!
The cutting of hair; the torturing of hair!
Helmets!
The drying of hair!
Helmets!
Sweepings of hair. The hair chute, for the
sweepings, leading down into the basement.
The air vent, leading upstairs,
right into my bedroom,
bringing me every word of conversation
that roiled out of that gynocracy!

At school I reeked of hair product,
pomades for the elderly,
lotions for the elderly.
I smelled of corn plasters and Barbicide!

In those first years of the shop, Lil's had Icelandic immigrant customers born in the 1860s. Lil and my mother reshaped their yellow-straw mops from what were virtually seventeenth-century Lutheran styles into the coiffures they needed to assimilate into modern Canadian culture.

LIL'S beauty shop

LILLIAN EYOLFSON
HERDIS MADOIN
Hair Styling Experts
Quality Permanents
All Methods
Heat and Cold
Open all day Wednesday
PHONE 36 731
802 Ellice, cor. Arlington

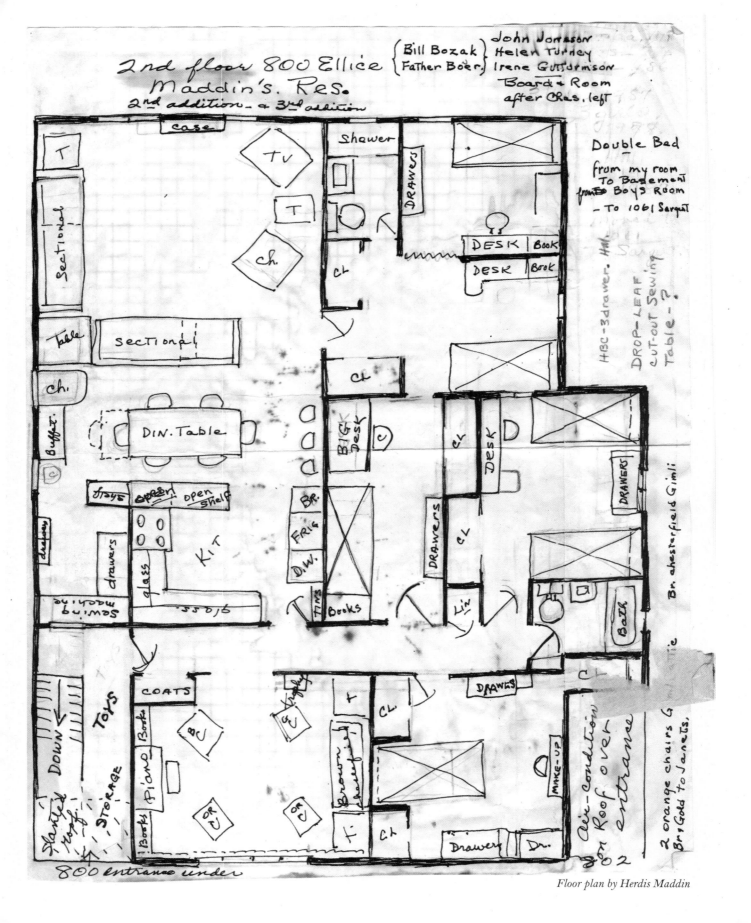

Floor plan by Herdis Maddin

Of girdles and talc.
Fur coats and purses.
The insides of purses!
The smells of female vanity and desperation.
I grew under their influences into what I am.

I will always love this shop.

White. Block. House.
White. Block. House.

I can't stop dreaming of this home.
It's changed since we sold it.
And it keeps changing in my dreams.
New shapes, similar, but confusing,
all the other addresses that appear
where 800 Ellice should be.
Smaller, longer, darker.
Lower, older, bigger.
But never just my … home.

Home. Home.
The dreams are sweet back home,
back home.
But the waking is bitter, bitter, bitter.

Bitterness.
Bitterness sweet as the cold of our winters.
We're the coldest city in the world.
What enchantments this cold offers up

My dreams were once haunted by the dead. Now it is architecture that has taken over my nocturnal preoccupations. Empty buildings through which I am doomed to wander, buildings missing every second board, buildings blasted by drafts, buildings bereft of human life, but still somehow packed with love, with sadness, with something latent. I ate at Inferno's restaurant in St. Boniface recently. The owner told me his place was haunted by the ghosts of strippers. Even their semi-transparent poles appear from time to time so these restless spirits may dance again.

I was the youngest of four children, and all my toys were hand-me-downs. Those toys, especially my zoo animals, were as packed with love and sadness as the empty architecture in which I am now nightly wandering. I didn't have the usual one-way relationship with these exotic plaster and lead creatures – it wasn't just me loving them. There was enough latent love in these animals, love soaked up by adoring years spent with my siblings, for the love to go both ways. So it is with the empty night rooms that love more than any room I could occupy by day. So it is with the poles and their dancers at Inferno's.

Winnipeggers drink more Slurpees per capita than the residents of any other city. I don't think we even need to use the *per capita* qualification – we just drink more Slurpees than any other city, period. A popular bumper sticker here identifies our province as 'Slurpitoba.'

ANCE AT NIGHT, HAPPYLAND, WINNIPEG, MAN.

to a person with the right attitude.
What exuberant lungfuls of fresh air
the city has for those
who want to scoop it up in their mouths.
Happiness!
Dazzling outdoor happiness
for anyone who cares to put on
a pair of mitts and embrace it.
Squeeze every last snowflake of joy from it.

Back in 1906, we Winnipeggers
built our own Happyland.
Our own Luna Park.
Our own Dreamland.
You'd never know it, but between these
west-end streets of Aubrey and Dominion,
between Portage Avenue and the Assiniboine,
sprawled the immense permanent
playground, teeming with oddity.
Wind-chilled roller coasters
and Ferris wheels enveloped themselves
in frost half the year.
A Happyland for us wintery Winnipeggers.
Happyland.
Keeping us happy.

All a dream, all a dream.
I need to wake up.
Keep my eyes open somehow.
I need to get out of here.

The 'Voice of K-Tel' was Bob Washington, a staff announcer at Winnipeg radio station CKRC. Wearing an apron, he once approached my table at the Old Spaghetti Factory, wielding a pot of coffee, to wait on me. In a depressing misreading of the situation, I assumed he had been fired by the radio station and forced into the service trade at seventy years old, when in fact – what a relief! – the Voice of K-Tel was merely working a celebrity fundraiser.

Rejected Narration: Our joyous *Winnipegwinter-sonnenwendespass!* (While writing the narration I had a brief, inappropriate crush on those learned-sounding German building-block words, this one meaning *Winnipeg mid-winter fun!*)

Herdis Maddin, c. 1932

Rejected dialogue:

MOTHER

Don't scratch the sofa. If you think I won't notice a new scratch, you're in for a very unpleasant surprise. I must say, you both have extremely clean fingernails. I noticed that right away. There's no reason labourers can't take pains with their grooming. My husband used to chew his nails. The only way I could get him to stop was to soak his fingers in turpentine. No one wants to be touched by hands that have been in somebody's germy mouth. In fact, you never know where hands have been. I have three mostly grown boys. And they think about the opposite … well, about the ladies. I hope they're ladies. Not many of them are these days. You can tell by their underthings. Some of them show their bellies. Now, you men, with your clean nails, wouldn't go to alleys for your fun. Would you? My sons might pay more attention to good advice if it came from men who work up a sweat at their job – who know what the score is. My own education was interrupted. I had to drop out of school because of the Indians. They were a jumpy bunch. They jumped on me every chance they got. I was a blond, you see. Finally I had enough. I got sick of all that jumping. So my school days were over. You're not supposed to say things about Indians now, but why be afraid of the truth? Remember to sweep up all that coffin dirt before you leave. Just because my husband is dead does *not* mean he's free to be messy.

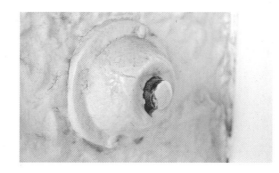

Out of here!
What if …
I film my way out of here?

It's time for extreme measures.
I need to make my own Happyland.
Back at 800 Ellice.

In commemoration of what
would have been my parents'
sixty-fifth wedding anniversary,
I sublet for one month
the house
in which I grew up.
Mother, as always,
is game for anything.
Eager is she to dip into
the past of her home.

I hire movers.
Tax deduction: I'm a filmmaker.

Only here can I properly recreate the
archetypal episodes from my family history.
Only here
can I isolate the essence of what
in this dynamic is keeping me in Winnipeg.
And perhaps once this isolation through
filmed re-enactment is complete,
I can free myself

Glaucoma-ravaged great-grandparents

Savage Genius

When George Toles and I finished this script about my strange plunge back into the mythically inchoate days of my childhood, and my city's childhood – days lived completely under the dominion of a fearsome maternal titan, years trembled out beneath the scented fist of my mother's gorgeous and glamorous dictatorship, an era when our town's craven populace cowered or tiptoed beneath the towering gams of this ferocious and all-seeing Matriarch who straddled like the Colossus our environs from above – I knew there was only one person alive, who had *ever* lived, who could play the role of my mother: Ann Savage.

Savage was, of course, while still living already immortalized for her toxically complex essaying of Vera, the most frightening femme fatale in the history of film noir, a role as much ferally attacked as performed, a role famously chewed up and spat out in just three furious days by this rage-fuelled actress in the most famous Poverty Row picture of all time, Edgar G. Ulmer's 1945 masterpiece, *Detour*. Bette Davis is reported to have been terrified by Savage's turn in this film, fleeing into the foyer of the theatre at its Poverty Row premiere to hide behind a potted palm lest she encounter this wrathful new thesp on her own malevolent, low-budget turf.

Now, after long and careful wooing by telephone, I had miraculously coaxed Miss Savage out of a fifty-one-year retirement to come up to unlikely and frosty Winnipeg to star in my movie. This feat I likened to tricking Garbo herself out in front of a movie camera after her decades in hiding, for when you think of it, Savage was indeed the Garbo of the modern American independent film world. She had been for a seeming eternity a woman seen only in fleeting glimpses, not in blurry snaps of a shrunken sunglassed shade as was the secretive Swede, but beheld by generations of ardently admiring young directors as the same twenty-four-year-old raw matter of studio pulchritude, frozen forever in *Detour*'s mid-forties, striding up and down the bewitched branches of time with the eternal vigour that cult martyrdom bestows as a consolation upon its unfairly marked-down gods and goddesses.

Unfairly, I say, because close inspection of Savage's work in *Detour* reveals a talent of incredible range that transcends cultiness; she plays hard-boiled, vulnerable, gutter sexy and posh, pitiable and psychotic, and even, ultimately and most astonishingly, sympathetic. Savage received her only acting training under Max Reinhardt during his thirties exile in Hollywood. This great Austrian maestro stressed naturalism in fantastic settings, and his occult curriculum made his apt pupil a perfect fit for Ulmer – and a half-century later the object of my most covetous dreams when I got it into my head that I just had to commit my mother's plausibly pretzelly personality to film.

The most unknown aspect of Ann is that she had a fine ear for music – was *very* moved by it the *instant* she heard it, even in the late years. She cried for three days when Ray Charles died. I believe her ear for music extended to the music of poetry, and good film dialogue. Toles' screenplay for *My Winnipeg* aspires to be, as *Detour*'s was, driven by dialogue that has very fine music in its word choices, rhythms, poetry, etc. Ann would not intellectualize these things, but she felt them, was deeply moved – it was this music that galvanized her responses, her performance. But she spoke off-camera with the same crackling music, that same staccato patter that scores her best movies. In fact, she showed up in Winnipeg spitting rivets, styling hard and fast conversations out of another, more lyrical era for my own awed and musically starved ears! 'That doesn't cut any ice with me!' was her favourite way of telling me to think of a better solution to an on-set problem.

Surprisingly, in her World War I pin-up days, Savage was primarily a leggy girl as opposed to a cleavage, back or face model – *lots* of exposed gams for Ann! And she was still so leggy at the end of her life that nobody ever realized she was only five foot three. When she was n set or out to dinner, people couldn't help but comment on how beautiful she looked.

Savage came from a time when faces, especially faces in luminous, silvery close-up, counted most. And even after a half-century away from the movies she still had hoarded within her mien a wealth of this dazzling currency. As in her pre-war screen tests at MGM, her face during her visit to Winnipeg, seventy years later, seized

the camera, arrested it and literally loaded up even the cheapest new film-stock emulsions with quantities of silver not used in Hollywood since the forties. Shocking was the power of her visage still, at age eighty-seven, enhaloed as it was in eerie ectoplasms, her presence an uncanny *it* imperiously demanding its rightful third dimension as it spectrally wafted – no, loomed threateningly – out toward her beholders.

One day, while we were shooting an homage to another Poverty Row Olympian, Ed Wood Jr., by placing Ann in front of a projected bison stampede worthy of *Glen or Glenda*, our fog machine suddenly exploded. Through the panicky billows that enshrouded every crew member, and led by the cowardly director himself, we scattered in every direction. I remember seeing a pair of long and silvery legs, sultry and sinuous, disembodied by the ersatz clouds that hung everywhere, make their way through orphaned shoes toward the detonated piece of equipment loudly sparking and sputtering amidst the darkling chaos of our set. These legs of phosphorus squared off against the smouldering machine, as if to intimidate all the smoke back into its rioting source. Calmly, an elegant, bioluminescent hand reached down beneath the low ceiling of spume and unplugged the contraption from its wall socket. And there, in the clearing air, stood Ann Savage, straddling tall the charred wreckage – sixty feet tall, I swear! – an imperishable leviathan divinity, hers the only dignity intact after this disturbing cataclysm, and not just intact but increased manifold and frighteningly, increased by the factor of all our dignities just slain by poltroonery; her face as big as any on Rushmore, but refulgent with *it*, numinous with its *it*-ness, radiating out past mortal frontiers into the infinities and eternities of film that only its fearsome gods can comprehend.

Portage Avenue

from the heinous power
of family and city and
escape once and for all.

In addition to shooting everything,
I keep a meticulous logbook
charting this strange plunge back in time.

It's 1963-ish, a time I believe most likely
to conceal the key to all the memories and
feelings that enervate me to this day.

In my old living room,
Mother puts everything back just as it was.
The old black-and-white TV in one corner,
the planters, the crummy sofa,
the comfy chair.
For one month
I get to sleep in my old bedroom,
the letters YUG still carved
dyslexically upon its door
so Santa will know I'm there.
Everything is exactly the same
as in my childhood.

The scope of this experiment
excludes my father
and I decide to keep him out of the formula.
My mother, missing him terribly
since his death some thirty years ago,

1963 was the height of 'metrophobia' in Winnipeg. All its seven boroughs, which had fused into 'Unicity' three years earlier, were now xenophobically plotting against one another, with Mayor Stephen Juba the dastardly pipesman calling a tune of discord. Citizen regarded citizen with increasing suspicion, wary that he be an interloper from St. Norbert, Headingly or St. Boniface. All of this was forgotten by 1972, buried in a time capsule beneath the Centennial Concert Hall.

Dream Diary: As a child I found out my father had a secret family, another whole life, in a house just one block away. A real-life character out of 'Wakefield,' but with kids, and my dad was happier with these children than he was with us. I spied on them through the window as they dined, and I marvelled at their harmony. Then I discovered that my mother had the same secret family. Not just one but both of my parents had parallel lives elsewhere, together, with happier and better kids – a Mr. and Mrs. Wakefield, although I don't think this is what Nathaniel Hawthorne had in mind at all when he wrote that great tale of deadbeat paternity. Both my mom and dad were much happier one block away. Still, they had to return regularly to dreary us, the criminal children.

Cameron, also an A+ student, an intercollegiate high-jump champion and science prodigy as well. At age fourteen he built a pirate radio station, broadcasting out into the neighbourhood from our garage till the police shut down his subversive programs featuring pro-Castro manifestos, bobby-soxer music and a variety of *Mad Magazine*–inspired burp jokes. He had repurposed his flying-saucer-shaped toboggan to serve as his antenna – the police confiscated it. He also built from scratch a hi-fi amp and turntable that I use to this day, outfitted the house with what felt like a Jetsons-era intercom system and wired our phones to broadcast music from their earpieces so that all our conversations might be scored with Top 40 hits. Inspired by strange impulses, he once threw his bicycle licence plate so high in the air above our backyard it disappeared, then he suddenly hopped on the balloon-tired, single-speed bike from which he had just detached the plate and pedalled all the way to our summer cottage at Loni Beach, over sixty miles from the city, a feat unheard of in that golden age of family station-wagon commutes.

Ross, yet another A+ student sibling, yet another high-jump champion and, by acclamation, the heir to my mother's title of Greatest Artist in the Family, perennially winning city-wide drawing and painting contests – his oil-crayon depiction of snowplows at rest, completed at age eleven, was by the time of my birth framed and hanging in the living room as an exemplar of Maddin plastic-arts mastery. I really loved this piece and love it still. Ross was also the sole wielder of the family's 8mm movie camera during his brief mania for recording Ellice Avenue life during the first two years of my life – this eerily dark pre-adolescent cinematography earning him, a half-century later, an 'additional camera' credit in the tail roll of *My Winnipeg*.

My dog Toby profoundly and regularly soiled the thick layers of newspapers on my bedroom floor with his waste. I hated picking up after Toby, but with Florient, that Space Age air freshener, that olfactory palimpsest in a can, I never had to touch a single glossy dropping or drenched paper. The revolutionary flowery freshness brewed up by modern science simply buried the smells of these once-acrid products of the wilful pet, and I slumbered sweetly each night in my room, a veritable synthetic garden of delicious odours.

Janet was a straight-A student who also happened to be the fastest woman in Canada while she was still in high school, at age seventeen ranking fourth in the world in the 200-metre. Whenever people in town heard my name, they asked me if I was related to her. http://www.halloffame.mb.ca/honoured/1987/jNeale.htm

In the shadow of all this sibling accomplishment, I was the triumphantly inert protagonist in my own modest story of achievement, logging more hours on the couch in front of the TV than anyone else in the history of sloth. My siblings and parents, never capable of resting, were like Futurist paintings, a blurry bustle of component parts – of doors opened and closed around my sofa; the rashly tallied human sum of lessons; practices and after-school jobs rushed after; rapid footsteps on the stairs that made the television hard to hear; the frequent wash of headlights on the ceiling. Nothing paused for long near me or the set, and only Toby, perpetually asleep on the furnace grate in the kitchen, and my grandmother, sitting in her dark eternal profile one floor below, could match the sweet dull comfort of my days.

lobbies strongly for his inclusion.
We settle on a compromise –
I pretend we've had him exhumed
and reburied in the living room beneath a
mound of earth concealed by the area rug.
This seems to buy her off,
for the time being anyway.

For the re-enactments that concern me,
I hire actors to play my brothers and sister.
Finding these actors isn't hard.
In fact, I'm able to get substitutes
that bear uncanny resemblances
to the vintage originals.

My sister Janet,
who in 1967 was a Pan-Am Games
gold medallist and is now a member
of the Manitoba Sports Hall of Fame.
My brother Cameron,
who died in 1963 at the age of sixteen.
My brother Ross.
Always big man on campus.
My dog Toby –
lived to be eleven and never
successfully house-trained –
to be played by my girlfriend's dog,
Spanky.
Actors for them all,
except Mother.

Once we finished the last stage of construction in the winter of 1959, thereby doubling the size of our block house at 800 Ellice, we were at full capacity. Eight people: parents, kids, Aunt Lil and Grandma. And Toby.

But dream homes never stay full for long. Soon, one place setting at a time was removed from the dining room table.

1963: Death of Cameron
1966: Janet moves to B.C.
1967: Death of Toby
1968: Ross moves to Regina
1970: Death of Grandma
1977: Death of Dad
1986: Death of Lil

Over the years we had boarders – including NHL Hall of Famer Gump Worsley, briefly – who filled for a time a few of the bedrooms as they emptied out, but mostly the vast and vacant house was mine to ramble through and occupy as I saw fit: a perfect locale for eternities of silent daydreaming and solitary mischief.

1987: Sale of 800 Ellice to Tam Nguyen, who opens Tam Custom Tailor. Tam is a marvellous person, a My Lai Massacre survivor and tailor to the stars: Philip Seymour Hoffman, Catherine Keener, Patrick Swayze, etc. He is the same age as me, has replaced me in my old bedroom without missing a beat and makes me, a mere filmmaker, feel pretty flaky because while I send out into the art-house world my little semi-surrealist autobiographies he does such noble charity work in Winnipeg's Vietnamese community, sending hard-earned money back to his old country to build schools.

I was born the very day that television broadcasting began in Winnipeg, and I was brought home from the hospital the same day as our new TV set. We were plopped down face-to-face on the living room carpet and left alone to stare at each other. There, in the endless solitude of preschool daytimes, the two of us enjoyed a long and happy codependence. I needed the TV to tell me of the world, when to laugh, at what and how hard, and the kind of hair I would have at forty; and the TV, for its part, needed me to change the channel — needed my hands and dandelion-stem wrists to twist its knob to an American show the instant a Canadian one, with its lousy lighting and acoustics recognizable even to a toddler, came on. It was a symbiotic friendship that thrummed along for years, both of us growing in each other's cathode gaze — the TV growing in channel selection, me growing ever more supine, and developing new ways of being supine on the sofas, until I was as good as deboned by many eons of idleness spent in unbroken companionship with my dearest pal, both of us oblivious to whatever parents and siblings gathered around us to watch. It wasn't till my sister noticed one of us masturbating in front of the unblinking stare of the other that our perhaps too-close relationship was called into question. And after the only family summit ever held on my account, the television and I were separated in an attempt to chasten the terms of our bond. On my fifteenth birthday I was given a brand-new portable colour set for personal use in my bedroom. The intervention worked — I completely forgot about my old beloved in the living room, and my family could watch its shows in peace without me.

At the last second,
the woman who sublets this place to me
decides she doesn't want to leave.
She puts a bit of a damper on things.

Experiment seems to be going well.
We start with something easy
the first few hours and everyone,
the hired actors, Mother,
the strange lady who won't leave her house,
are all comfortable enough
in the old living room
to gather around the TV to watch
the only television drama
ever produced in Winnipeg.

LEDGEMAN

Don't try to sweet-talk me.
Talk talk talk, all you do is talk.
I'm going to do it for real this time.

It was a daily TV drama called *Ledgeman*,
and my mother's been the female lead in this show
since 1956.

MOTHER

Don't think they don't know
you're a coward and a baby
who has to get his own way.
You're looking pretty cocky

In the early nineties, *Ledgeman* was bumped by vpw to late night by the new program *Dances with Cougars*.

Rejected dialogue:

MOTHER

If you want to quit your job and lie around like a pasha from now on, I'll buy extra pillows for the sofa. I'll pick up your soiled clothes and do the laundry if you're too busy. You won't have to lift a finger. I will never again accuse you of stealing change from my purse. I didn't mean it when I said I missed the car you wrecked more than I miss your father. I take that back. I miss them both the same. It is for you, not me, to decide if the lawn needs mowing. Even if it looks like a jungle out there and the neighbours complain, I won't ask. I will hire a boy, or do it myself. Get up whenever you like, morning or afternoon, and choose a girl with messy hair to have your babies with. I won't ask to see the marriage licence. I'll trust you to look after that in your own good time. And you don't need a haircut. It's just a little mangy. I'll buy you a comb and leave it on your dresser.

(Son decides to come in.)

Why would you stand out there wearing socks with holes in them? I'm not going back on my word, but you'll never have to worry about me speaking to you again. I'll stay in my room until something happens and then you can put me next to your father under the floor. Maybe then you'll be happy, knowing that you've killed the two of us. And the law can't touch you. Then you can have the run of the place, and make your women moan and put out their dirty tongues and laugh at your poor dead mother as they toss their ratty things everywhere.

(Son returns to the ledge.)

Now what? So that's how it is. What more do you need? Your dead brother's room? It's yours. And you don't need to return my shoe stretchers. If my shoes are pinching, it's not your worry. At my age, I can lose a few toes and hardly miss them. From now on, you make the rules, and I'll abide by them. Tell me how to love you, and I'll do it.

My mother, in drag

now that you've given me shingles
and made me lick dirt
for the television people.

Every day – the show runs at noon –
the same oversensitive man
takes something the wrong way,
climbs out on a window ledge
and threatens to jump.
And every day,
his mother appears at the nearest window
and tells him to remember
all the reasons for living.

MOTHER

In spite of what you think,
you have *never* been a
disappointment to me.
When you were a child model
for Hudson's Bay,
I was so full of pride
I could hardly breathe.
That little checked suit,
not a hair out of place.

By the end of each episode,
the son is convinced to come in to safety,
but the next day
he's back out there again.
Mother has never missed a day

Guy Maddin, child model

39

On our coldest days, we Winnipeggers are enveloped in great shrouds of car exhaust, blinded by billowing rills of chimney smoke and miniature cloudlets of breath. Trains crash audibly in the whiteness; snippets of conversation hang in the silvery air, orphaned by the erasures of all speaking people; from curling bonspiels on the river, rocks collide like thunder, and brooms, sweeping, swirl out of the void; a newsstand appears – a woman buys a paper then vanishes, swallowed up in the fog – before the whole stand evaporates too. The more Winnipeggers forget, the more their genetic memories push through the fog.

During our nightly peregrinations, we Winnipeggers visit the cityscapes of both worlds, the past and the present, which exist contemporaneously. The people and buildings that were once here but are now gone are allowed to coexist with those that remain. We remember equally what happened today and long ago: no temporal distinction is made, and therefore no qualitative distinction either. Delightful recollections of childhood and morbid adult reminiscences are weighted equally. Buildings long-razed reappear; our cemeteries have an unstable population that rises and falls each night.

Some people obey memories without realizing it, and the sidewalks seem to have been laid out along invisible ancient trading routes or hunting paths, still winding around long-gone trees and shrubs. The walkways along Main Street honour these pathways in the tortuous manner with which their cobblestones were laid for the 1999 Pan-Am Games. (Long live that year's Canadian baseball hero, Stubby Clapp!) But other, straighter sidewalks are still negotiated as if they wind around old obstacles, and the gait of our pedestrians sometimes gives them the aspect of hunters creeping in a silent, vigilant crouch – sleep-hunters perhaps, obeying ancient impulses, crawling deeper into the city until completely buried, never to re-emerge. Then, like a neurology patient with no short-term memory, Winnipeg is astonished to find itself as old as it is. It catches its surprisingly old reflection in store windows, and trembles there in shock.

Winnipeg is an oubliette.

in the fifty years the show
has been broadcast.

Surprisingly, after half a century
of acting on TV, Mother is resistant
to playing the role of herself
in this exciting experiment of mine,
which could actually not just
unlock the secrets of a family
but create a whole new genre of film.
She's always been stubbornly resistant
to my most important ideas.
Just to show me who's boss,
she'll forget her line or transpose its syllables –
anything to destroy a take.
I just know she's doing it to be difficult.

We fight on-set.
But her refusal to acknowledge the real past
becomes scientifically significant, I think.
Very telling.

This is going to be a good month,
the month of my great escape.
It's a singular chance, this month.
Who gets to vivisect his own childhood?

The first full scene up is the straightening of
the hall runner, something we did
every exasperating day of my childhood.

Under the aegis of Tam Nguyen, the hallway of 800 Ellice is now runnerless.

Guinness World Records lists the longest recorded heart stoppage (of a person later revived) at three hours and forty minutes: it was Winnipegger Jean Jawbone, who, at the age of twenty, was brought back to life by a team of twenty-six medical staff using peritoneal dialysis in our Health Sciences Centre on January 8, 1977. Years later, I heard the poor unlucky died in a house fire.

An unbelievable source of frustration
for everyone, for the rug could never be
straightened out no matter how much
anyone pulled from either end.
And Mother always nagged from the sidelines.
The actors put in a limp performance,
displaying little affect,
and it's me behind the camera who gets
frustrated instead of them.
An inspired Spanky tries to help out
by getting in the way
just as dead, dead Toby always did.
But almost none of the data collected in this
re-enactment will be of any use.

But still, it's working.
Mother is in the moment.

Never underestimate the tenacity of a
Winnipeg mother.

The year 1957 saw Winnipeg embroiled
in the scandal of the Wolseley Elm, a tree
growing out of the centre of Wolseley Avenue,
surrounded by a curb and a fringe of grass
that *Ripley's Believe It or Not!* declared
was the smallest park in the world.
In 1957, the city assigned a crew to
remove the elm. In the ensuing standoff,
a dozen elderly neighbourhood women

The giant triple-trunked tree was planted in 1859 by a girl named Mary Anne Good who lived on a prairie farm near the bank of the Assiniboine. Little did she suspect the sapling she nurtured would be doomed one century later by the razing of one football stadium and the construction of a new one, both of these structures not only decades but miles away from the one-time site of her farm. On August 22, 1953, a parade crawling down Portage Avenue, led by French movie star Corinne Calvet waving from a white convertible, marshalled the Winnipeg Blue Bombers football club from their old home at Osborne Stadium (1935–52; capacity 7,800) to the new Winnipeg Stadium, just north of the Polo Park Racetrack on St. James Street. (A mere twenty minutes after the opening of the new stadium, Miss Calvet nipped over to the nearby Airport Drive-In Theatre at Century and Ellice to preside over the Winnipeg opening of her new Hollywood picture, *Rope of Sand*, a William Dieterle diamond-mine adventure also starring Burt Lancaster, Peter Lorre and Mike Mazurki.) The new stadium shifted heavy gameday automobile traffic down Wolseley Avenue, which even to this day offers miles of pavement without traffic-light interruption. City councilmen and other hurried drivers demanded the removal of the tree. In addition to the dynamite that eventually killed the tree, anonymous local vandals had earlier tried dousing the tree with gasoline and setting it ablaze, attacking the tree with saws and crowbars, and even adopting the KKK strategy of placing a rooster – that frightening organization's long-standing mascot and symbol of its vengeful pride – in its trunk. A prominent Winnipeg psychiatrist opined that such tree-haters were actually mad at society and not the beloved elm.

Noamie II: 1919 Queer Trickery

My good friend and compatriot, the Night Mayor of Winnipeg, chose the 1919 General Strike as a topic for his first film, aptly titled *1919*. The strike's anniversary had long been celebrated as a holiday in the Gonick family house. Noam grew up obsessed with its history, so much so that he felt he alone could reconfigure it, setting the movie inside a Chinese barbershop/bathhouse named Wong's, speculating that the Strike Committee had held half-clothed meetings in the sauna and that the real, daytime Mayor of Winnipeg had been held captive in its humid confines after the Workers of the World united.

This idea came to Noamie as he had his Hebraic curls pomaded by Bill the Barber, the octogenarian buzz-cut specialist we all visited during that spell. The joint also had takeout frozen dim sum, fireworks, a tailor shop and two steam rooms: one for families and both genders on the ground floor, and a basement lair that was male-only. Occasionally I would catch an ogre leering from the depths while I was waiting for my turn in the barber's chair.

The building was ancient and no doubt an interesting place to hide out during the historic riots that took glorious place mere blocks away. The complex was burned down one cold February night (in late bareback season) just a few years ago by an insane male flight attendant. The elderly patrons, wearing nothing but their towels, were winched off the roof in a fire-truck bucket. The next morning, the remains of the sauna were an ice fortress, giant stalactites drooping from the telephone wires. Another piece of history to be levelled into a parking lot come spring.

The newspaper headlines announced that the birthplace of the General Strike had been burned down by the Indian Posse, an all-Native street gang. They were wrong on both accounts, but myth-savvy Noam would later put the Indian Posse on the silver screen in his film *Stryker*, an important filmic depiction of contemporary urban Aboriginal life.

Bible Kampf: Noam Gonick's unfinished film. The story fixates on Abraham's self-circumcision in a fit of religious madness. Noam and I have resolved to somehow anyhow complete this film by the time this book is out of the print shop.

encircled the tree arm in arm
to fend off the city workers' buzz saws.
Within minutes the police had arrived,
paddy wagons and all, for the old biddies.
A crowd gathered.
'If they want to chop down this tree,'
said one woman,
'they're going to have to chop us down first.'
In the end the matter was settled peacefully
by newly elected mayor Stephen Juba,
who pulled up in his Cadillac
and sent the workers home.
Later that week, vandals,
obviously working for the city,
blew up the tree with dynamite.

What if?
What if City Hall ever listened to
the wishes of the people?

1919.
Returning soldiers and police on the right.
Our workers on the left.
The drama of our city's
most glorious moment.
The 1919 General Strike.
The clash of the marchers.
Their grand parades surging from
each direction,
meeting in the middle.

My grandmother's earliest memory is of the time the roof of the sod hut in which she was born caught fire. Everyone scrambles to put out the blaze. Pails of fresh cow's milk are closer to hand than water for the farm help and so the flames are doused with these. From inside her crib, my little grandma sees the milk pouring through the cracks in the ceiling down onto her blankets – an indoor milk rain.

Stephen Juba, the most celebrated and beloved mayor in Canadian history, owed much of his long career to his plan, renewed each election campaign, to completely cover Winnipeg in a giant Plexiglas dome that would keep the city free of snow in the winter, free of mosquitoes in the summer. He allowed rumour to suggest it would also serve as a cloak of invisibility against Russian nuclear attack, a fear the Ukrainian Juba felt with particular acuity. The like-minded electorate never gave him less than 80 percent of the popular vote.

*Preparatory collage
by Jonah Corne*

Meeting where?
On this day,
in front of St. Mary's Academy for Girls.

St. Mary's Academy for Girls,
where the quaking little princesses
of the middle class
tremble out their fathers' fear of workers.
Fear that workers may actually
get paid fairly someday.

But the workers are not to be denied.
Neither police truncheon nor
the wealth of the bourgeoisie
can stall their determination.
The newspapers paint the workers as
Bolshevik rapists, which galvanizes
the girls' worrisome fathers into a
frenzy of paranoia and sets the nuns,
those ever-opiating nuns,
foolish as the turkeys they raise,
puffing up into a gobbling panic.
Such was the crucible of the continent's
labour movement here in Winnipeg.
Brave men, doing what had to be done.
Teaching the next generation to
throw off its girlish fears of the inevitable.

The workers.
The workers' night school,

In my recollection, the only remotely Oedipal episode involving my father and his mother was the time he sleepwalked to the foot of her bed and urinated on her feet.

Now I dream I find my father, dead these thirty years, wandering lost in Winnipeg's ice fogs. Here we're the same age: two middle-aged men, together groping our way in the bright iridescence. I take his arm in mine and kiss him lightly upon his long-closed lashes, a soft touch over both good eye and glass, and drowsily guide him home to bed.

St. Mary's Academy and College

Directed by THE SISTERS OF THE HOLY NAMES OF JESUS AND MARY

Preparatory collage by Guy Maddin

and some of their most eager students
sleepwalk right out to the barricades
to meet their new teachers.
What they want they know not,
but they're going to get it.
And our city will be at the forefront
of the workers' rights movement
for the rest of the century.

You can feel the spirit of labour still
whenever you walk around
St. Mary's Academy at night.
You can still see the impotent old fence,
now snow-buried, that once tried to keep
those heroic Bolsheviks at bay.

Now, a single sleepwalker re-marches
the same historic route the strikers took
past the school. Is he remembering
with his blood those long-ago days of
excitement or is he just another sleepwalker
jingling his keys in his pocket?
He's barely noticed by anyone at St. Mary's.
He is as invisible as I am otherwise.
Maybe it is I.

The closest I ever got to St. Mary's
Academy for Girls:
I can remember getting lost as a
three-year-old who rode off from home

In this collage, Jonah Corne attempted to assign culpability for the Great Flood of 1950 to the Winnipeg minstrel suffrage movement of 1915.

Producer Jody Shapiro and I attempted to construct a complicated Slavko Vorkapich–inspired montage wherein we suggest that all Catholic schoolgirls are born like so many sea monkeys from droplets of melting orange popsicles. The concept was a bust, but the afternoon spent sharing popsicles with the test subjects was a consolation.

Sister Renée updates her Facebook status

on the seat of my little green dump truck and
ending up on the grounds of St. Mary's –
forbidden territory for a boy.
Soon, I was surrounded by solicitous
schoolgirls who coddled me, teased me,
held my hand, pressed me into their blouses
and kissed me in a kind of competition
over me that ended only
with the arrival of a big nun.
Now my encounters with the students
of this fenced-in school are limited only to
little lunchtime sightings. The girls like to
smoke at Munson Park across the street.

Delinquent girls.
Nothing stokes
my mother's engines more.
Well, delinquent girls are all in the past
for me, Mother!
It's time to get back to work.
Back to the task of disentangling myself
from this town.

One scene I was really anxious
to get at was the recreation of the time
my sister hit a deer on the highway
coming back from Kenora.
I felt at the time my mother
really overreacted.
I need to view this episode again.

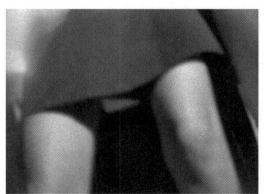

Was it my sister's fault?
Was it my mother's?

JANET (*in tears*)

Mother, I had an accident.

MOTHER

With the car? There's no such thing as accidents.

JANET

I ran into a deer.

MOTHER

On a country road, I suppose. And just what were you doing out there?

JANET

I told you. A track-team party.

MOTHER

Out in the woods. With boys who can run faster than you, I wager.

JANET

The deer wasn't dead – and I stood there crying until a driver stopped.

MOTHER

And what did he want?

JANET

He helped me, Mother. He got a tire iron and put the deer out of his misery.

With the invaluable help of Winnipeg-based collage-party doyen Paul Butler, I arranged for some of my favourite artist friends to fashion storyboards for me during *My Winnipeg*'s pre-production. I felt the input of other sensibilites would help me break stale old habits I had acquired assembling movies over the past two decades. Paul threw together a total of five collage happenings for the film. Two were held in Winnipeg, two in nearby Gimli and one in San Francisco. In each case, Paul supplied some X-acto blades, some vintage LPs and some fireworks to shake up routine; I supplied a stack of old magazines, a case of bourbon and a list of suggested subjects culled from Winnipeg's history. Then we let the artists go crazy. This army of visionary helpers, who really taught me through this convivial creative process how to loosen up my camera and find the mad truth inside the literal one, included Jeff Funnell (JF), Meeka Walsh (MW), brothers Evan (EJ) and Galen Johnson (GJ), Caelum Vatnsdal (CV), Brad Phillips (BP), Jonah Corne (JC) and Carl Matheson (CM). Paul (PB) and I (GM) chipped in as well.

Brown's Creek (GM)

GM

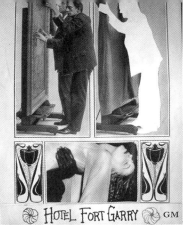

JF

HOTEL FORT GARRY GM

JF

MW

PB

JF

CV

CARBERRY DESERT GM

BEARS ON BROADWAY GM

GM

GM

BP

PB

Remember? PB

PB

MOTHER

Let's see the damage.

OUTSIDE. *Mother inspecting the fender.*

MOTHER

Now what do you have to say for yourself?

JANET

There's the deer fur and blood. And the
dent. Just like I said.

MOTHER

I wasn't born yesterday, dearie. I know all
about fur and all about blood. Where did
it happen? In the back seat?

JANET

Where did what happen?

MOTHER

The real party. Did he pin you down, or did you
just lie back and let nature take its course?

Mother, she knows how to read all the signs.
Those gentle substitutions for dark wishes.

MOTHER

Was it a boy on the track team or the man
with the tire iron?

JANET

Mother, you're not making any sense.
You sound like a crazy person.

Neil Young's first Winnipeg apartment was in the block at Hugo and Corydon, where, decades after Shakey had moved out to live his legend, I found myself with a drinking companion who slept in the rock great's former bedroom. There, I was almost accused of sexual assault in a misunderstanding that ironed itself out in about ten minutes.

Crimes! In the 1960s, owners of Birt Saddlery, a now-gone leather-goods store on Main Street, next to the Big 4 Sales and our new city hall, discovered a secret passage behind a bricked-over doorway in their basement. This passage led to a tunnel that once connected a jail in Birt's basement to the old city hall. Then someone realized the passageway was no simple thoroughfare. It was a long and narrow gallows, a place of execution. Buried beneath our peaceful twenty-first-century streets is a great, perfectly preserved chamber, lined with multiple nooses suspended above a corridor of trapdoors. A death chamber at the very core of our city. There are rumours, never proven, that this was an early attempt at privatizing capital punishment.

MOTHER

We'll see how crazy I am. I know what it's like out there. Every night, the same old story. Take that off, put this on, take this in, pull that out. Push, pull, roll over and done. Don't try my patience. Who did it?

The signs hiding in plain sight.

MOTHER

No innocent girl stays out past ten with blood on her fender.

JANET

It's my life. Not yours.

MOTHER

And who gave you that life?

JANET

I never asked for it.

MOTHER

I didn't either. Believe me. If I could have arranged to send you back and get one that knew how to behave herself, I would have. So help me God.

JANET

Well, I wish you had. I'd rather be an orphan.

Janet Maddin at the 1967 Pan-Am Games in Winnipeg.

MOTHER

Don't tempt me. Every night I take a
good hard look at my pills. One little push
is all I need. It was the man with the tire
iron. He saw the fur and the blood and
that was that.

JANET

It wasn't like that. You weren't there.

MOTHER

Did he pay you?

JANET

No. What do you think I am?

MOTHER

So what did all the tears for the deer
accomplish? All they did was put you in
the mood. For the other.

JANET

I'll never see him again.

MOTHER

Of course you won't. It took him all of five
minutes to see what you are.

My sister hit and killed a deer.
My mother sees through this euphemism,
for it is a euphemism – everything that
happens in this city is a euphemism.
Mother understands in a second

Rejected dialogue:

JANET
So tell me, Mother. What am I?

MOTHER
There's no proper word for it. (*Gives her a douche
bag.*) After you've finished, go to your room.
(*Grabs her face.*) Next time a deer comes along
and you hit it, just back up and drive over
it again. Otherwise, you can forget about track.
Soon you won't be fit to run anywhere. And
don't imagine that there's anything you do
anywhere with anyone that I don't know about.

Mother, Assiniboine Park, c. 1935

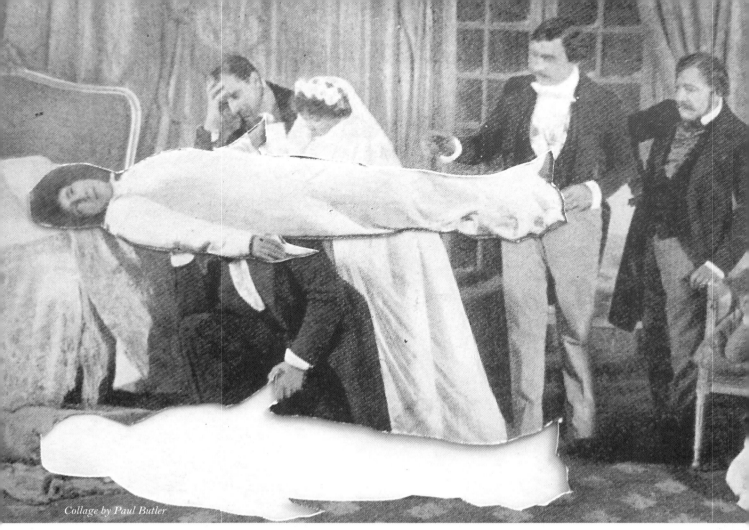

Collage by Paul Butler

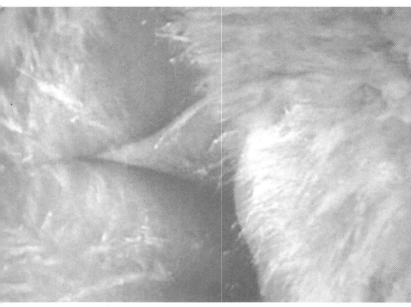

The Forks
beneath
the Forks!

what this deer blood and fur means,
and somehow she's right.
She can read our family and our civic secrets,
 our desire and our shame,
as easily as she can read a newspaper.
Mother –
maybe the most psychic of all Winnipeggers.
No matter where I am,
I can feel her watching me.
I can feel her hand on my shoulder
when I'm out sleepwalking,
guiding me back to my own bed.
I don't think it matters if she's
awake or asleep, living or dead,
she'll always know
exactly what I'm doing.

Winnipeggers have always been skilled
at reading past the surface and into the
hidden depths of their city.
On a small scale, we had
Curious Lou Profeta back in the 1930s.
He was known for despooking furniture
that people feared haunted.
The city once even hired him to
spiritually cleanse a streetcar
that was giving passengers the jitters.

Sir Arthur Conan Doyle
always cited Winnipeg as having the

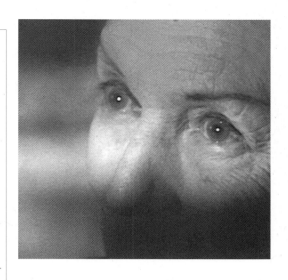

Rejected narration: Deer fur and blood: all this adds up to what our German immigrants call *schlechtverkehr*, or *bad traffic* – our Teutonic people's best euphemism yet for intercourse.

Winnipeg characters

Streetcar Stella rode Winnipeg's urban rail system from the 1930s till trolleys were removed from service in September of 1955, and, as a perhaps misguided public service, lubricated all vertical support poles inside the cars on her line with handfuls of her own saliva.

Bicycle Bob rode a penny-farthing all over town on inscrutable missions for four decades beginning in the 1890s. When the eccentric octogenarian finally passed away, slumped up against his wooden bike in his tiny, carton-lined Kennedy Street apartment, he was feted at an immense and lavish funeral, paid for by two levels of government, and which the premier, the mayor, the speaker of the house, provincial court judges and cabinet ministers attended.

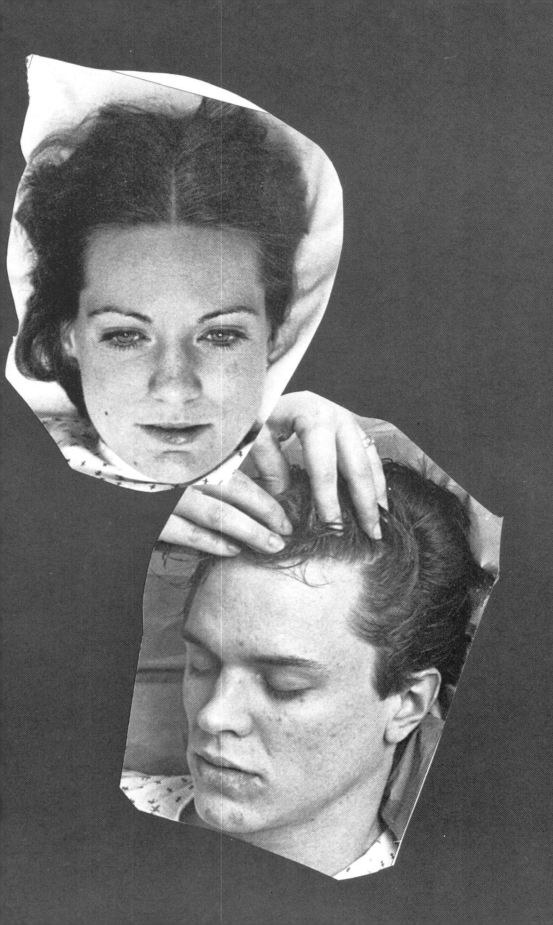

Collage by Carl Matheson

greatest psychic possibilities
of any city he had ever visited.
Possibly because of the lap,
the fur or the frost, etc.
But especially because of the Forks,
and the Forks beneath the Forks.

The First Nations people knew how to read
what Conan Doyle only sensed in this city,
for centuries burying their dead
as close as possible to the most powerful
confluence of our four rivers,
Red and Assiniboine,
Red and Assiniboine.

In the 1920s,
Thomas Glendenning Hamilton,
distinguished Winnipeg medical doctor
and politician,
held at his home
elaborately documented séances
in the hope of contacting his dead son.
These nocturnal confabulations
quickly spun out into the
viscous and cottony hallucinations
you see here.
Depictions of the city's
constantly waged war
between two worlds –
the one in which Winnipeggers

Thomas Glendenning Hamilton owned a
cottage just seven doors down from ours at Loni
Beach, one hour out of Winnipeg. My friend Sid
Swartz grew up next door to the Hamiltons
and was always spooked by the summer séances,
banshee howls, rappings, clairvoyances, trance
states, telekinetics, bell-ringings, visions and
teleplasmic manifestations transpiring in this
darkened cabin. Whenever I walked Spanky past
the place, sixty years later owned by the Millers
(a lovely family), the pug's hair, usually a relaxed
fawn nap, would stand on end and eerily undu-
late as though animated by *King Kong* demi-
urge Willis O'Brien.

live now and
the one they expect to inhabit in the future.

The most intriguing work in the
paranormal field here in Winnipeg
was led by medium Gweneth Lloyd
back in 1939, the same year she co-founded
what became eventually the
Royal Winnipeg Ballet.
She conducted a number of notorious
séances in which she danced out,
rather than spoke, the restless messages from the
denizens of the beyond.
The most famous of these meetings she
conducted at our provincial legislative
building, which also happens to be the
world's largest Masonic temple.
Secretly constructed along ancient occult
specifications in 1920 by our premier,
Rodmond P. Roblin, who along with his
entire cabinet were third-degree Masons.
That's the Greek god Hermes
atop our dome, disguised as the
Golden Boy by an armful of wheat,
our sleepy eyes never suspecting his
fearsome pagan power and
unlikely presence
in modern North America.

Gweneth Lloyd also helped to support the
Winnipeg Ballet Club financially, by contributing
horses' horoscopes to local racing magazines.

Saint Paul, Minnesota-based writer Jon Spayde's
poem from his collection, *My Manitoba*:

My Manitoba II
In the Manitoba Legislative Assembly bills
are reported out as dreams.
No. 282:
A bear shall lick the gold leaf
off the legs of the allegorical figure
of the Domestic Pleasures
on the Wheat Palace.
Ayes: 41
Nays: 3

Back in the 1980s, I would occasionally visit my good friend Dr. Dan Snidal, the Associate Dean of Medicine at the University of Manitoba, and accompany him on his daily rounds of the school at the Health Sciences Centre, the hospital in the very heart of old Winnipeg, butted up against the streets named after those pioneer madams. I loved these little jaunts with the doctor: there was always something intriguing inside this medicined world of his. With his long strides – Danny was a loping six foot seven – these institutional tours were always brisk, leaving me wanting more, and my guide's accounts of what I was about to see at each upcoming stop, pitched for the layman I was, were always limned out in an unselfconscious poetry, the result, probably, of my friend's attempts to find just the right metaphors to illustrate in simple strokes, and thus make contagious, his own enthusiasm for the infinite complexities of human pathology.

My favourite of the wards we frequented, though also the saddest, was a large, overcrowded room of patients suffering from the strangest memory disorder – I can't, ironically, remember its name. (I keep thinking of it as Mulchy's Syndrome, but can find no record of such an affliction anywhere, so perhaps I'm misremembering the name.) Dr. Snidal claimed that Winnipeg had the best Mulchy's Syndrome research centre in the world.

The patients beset by this illness – and this is the remarkable thing – live in a constant state of déjà vu. We've all experienced déjà vu, that vaguely pleasant and unpleasant certainty that we have already somehow experienced the very moment in which we are now occupied, and that this earlier incident, completely identical to the current one right down to the most minute emotional and neurological details, haunts us now as some memory fixed in an uncertain and elusive past as something that *really* happened. Déjà vu has medically known causes, something to do with the cranial routes carrying new data and stored data getting crossed so that the new perceptions come to us as old – it's simple to explain away. And strange as it feels, it's a benign, if discombobulating, part of life.

Well, the patients in the Mulchy ward, because of permanently crossed neural pathways, live in a constantly disorienting state of déjà vu. Absolutely every new sensation that comes to them arrives as something they have already experienced at some slippery point in the past. Nothing is new to these Winnipeggers! Everything they experience they have experienced before, or so they believe. This is no *Groundhog Day* – no, this is something far more

paralyzing. Every sentence uttered to them they have heard before. Even messages carrying the most emotionally traumatic news – the death of a loved one, the 9/11 tragedy – are greeted with an annoyance at the stale-dated, instantly redundant report. The recipients of such sad bulletins are unmoved, so convinced are they that their loved ones have already died, that they have already been informed of the passings in exactly the same manner as now, but some time ago. The emotions usually attending such events are left forever undischarged in the patient. What, if anything, happens to all this potentially backed-up feeling is not known.

The confusion created in the poor convalescents by these crossed wires quickly ramifies. Even the act of remembering the earlier experience becomes an experience lived before. These people falsely remember the remembering, and then in turn falsely remember that ersatz recollection, and so on, until a counterfeit past telescopes behind them. For these wretched Winnipeggers, nothing new is even possible.

The memories pile up far too quickly to permit even a spurious species of nostalgia to attach itself to them. The patients live mostly in an unfeeling state – no affect and no fear – for nothing can surprise them; nothing can even happen to them that hasn't already happened to them. But the fearlessness is not courage: it is merely an unimaginative lack of fear, an artifact of their querulous rote exhaustion with the city, its inhabitants and everything ever said here. The patients are not depressed, never suicidal. In fact, they have proven to be hardier than any other long-term residents at the HSC. Most even hold down jobs, though they are obviously limited by their emotional paralysis and their inability to determine properly their place in time. The CBC has been remarkably empathetic and supportive by hiring many of these syndrome sufferers; many of the afflicted have even risen to senior bureaucratic positions in management and accounting at that great and noble corporation.

Dr. Snidal estimated at the time of my first visit to the ward that for every one of these déjà vu–afflicted, there were perhaps a thousand more wandering the streets of our city undiagnosed. With the hypochondria typical of anyone having a new disease described to him, I instantly feared I too was persecuted by this ailment. But that was just the moment when I realized I have in fact always been tormented by its opposite, if maladies can have opposites. For I have, in fact – and I have found no other Winnipegger with whom to commiserate over this – always felt paralyzed by my own peculiar species of déjà vu. Unlike the hospital cases described above, who live life perpetually in the second half of the déjà vu experience, in the moment apparently but not actually already lived, I have a different problem: I always feel as if the moment in which I live shall be lived again, a second time.

Whenever one of life's enormous moments – the death of my father, the birth of my daughter – comes to me with all its attendant emotional demands, I never feel the event properly, at the right time or with the appropriate volume of passion. Perhaps I am simply overwhelmed, blowing a fuse at these instants, but it doesn't feel so. As Fate's wrecking ball whooshes toward my very soul, it seems like I have plenty of time to get my feelings right, that I have till much later to feel properly and that I'll only have to worry about my response then, when the great moment comes by again like a comet in its inexorable orbit. I feel that I will be able to grieve properly when my father dies again, a second time; that I will rejoice properly when my infant daughter is delivered to me again, that second time. I can't escape the conviction that everything will happen twice, and that this life is but the first time for everything, and – I repeat – I'll have plenty of time to experience all the heart-wringing emotions later, thoroughly, properly, redemptively. In fact, I'll be better equipped to do so now that I've had my life previewed for me during this first go-by. Sweet certitude!

Try as I might, I can't shake myself free of this strange conviction that I am living the front half of the déjà vu experience. I *know* it isn't true, but I *feel* it is, and feeling is more important than knowing. Even after having my cat put down recently, I asked the vet if a better diet and more exercise would prevent this fatal onset of feline diabetes next time – and I didn't mean next time I owned a cat, I meant next time I owned this very same cat. Kessa, I won't fail you a second time!

This life view of mine is as good as a disease. And even though I can find no other Winnipegger who admits to the same symptoms, I can't help but feel our streets must be thronged with those who feel just as I do. Here are citizens who have never gotten it right the first time, a city that has never gotten it right, never felt comfortable in its own moments, always postponed doing the right thing until some vague time in the future, a time that is a figment of two shorted-out nerves, two crossed Manitoba Hydro cables. Build a giant downtown mall or arena in spite of all prevailing expert opinion, but do so knowing we can get it right later. Allow our city to sprawl profligately in any direction a developer or politician wishes, but do so knowing the whole thing can be undone next time around! Allow visionary opportunity after visionary opportunity to slip away without fear, for those very same opportunities will arrive just as fresh again some other day, next time that enchanted comet swings by. Our whole past can be relived – next time perfectly. No worries about this time!

Another place Dr. Snidal used to take me was Brookside Cemetery, next to the grey, blustery runways of our international airport, where once a year he would preside over the interment of his medical-school cadavers – also the limbs amputated at Winnipeg's many hospitals. I could never get out of my mind the strangeness of these funerals, and I was drawn to them year after year, just the three of us there, Dr. Snidal, a generic pastor and me, standing over an oversized open grave. I couldn't help thinking again of our city's spiked incidence of Mulchy's Syndrome, its pathological déjà vu, and how these cadavers were experiencing, with feelings impossible to determine, their second funerals – for they must have all had memorial services before, at the time of their deaths. Here they were again, honoured, consecrated, living out the back half of twinned events, their burials. Closure – again! The back half of déjà vu. These were the dead versions of those CBC employees and others beset by that rum, chronic nothing-new-ness.

And I was represented at these funerals by the amputated limbs, those portions of people still living, still owning many years of life with which to accomplish all there is to do, but already having their first final rites. The second funeral for the owners of these limbs – real proper services, fully attended burials, when grief and fear will properly flourish – were years off. These amputated limbs were merely cast into the Brookside ground as part of that filmy, unimportant first unit of the paired phenomena of memory, the front half of déjà vu, the part that hasn't really happened yet and therefore doesn't really count for anything.

We here in Winnipeg live in this blithe relationship with conjoined past and future, and are

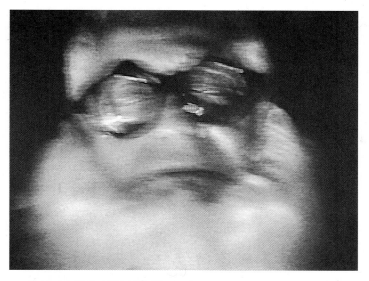

truly blessed – if we must be ravaged by some derangement – to have these benign infirmities as our masters! For if we aren't afflicted by some syndrome – either Mulchy's or my own – then we are passing our time in neurological states fixed somewhere in between these two opposites. No sooner do we see the future than we have already lived it! We're unflappable! Everything is history, unsurprising, already passed, but we are not only fearless of the future, we crave its arrival as an exalted opportunity to feel the Parousia of rising clouds beneath our feet.

Here, somewhere between two psychic extremes, the starting line and the finish, we rev our fearsome engines, our gaskets flapping wildly in the cosmic gale. We are precisely here – and everywhere else too, all at once! And we're fast! We are the benighted and benumbed, infantile with our Gnostic all-knowing 'something'! Yes, we have 'something,' and somehow we know it!

Winnipeg! Sweet, subconscious city!

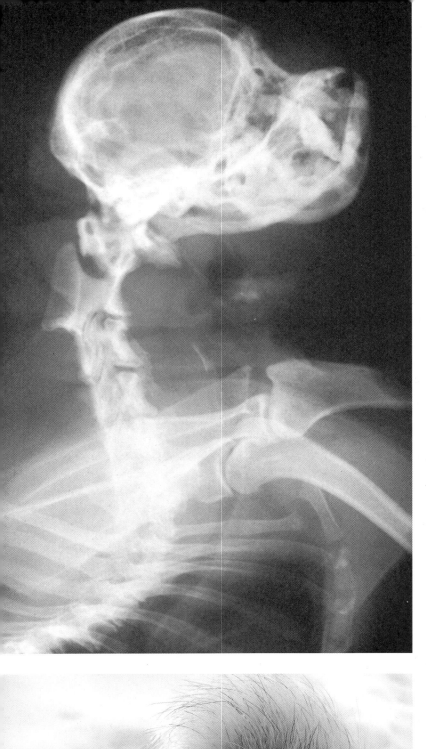

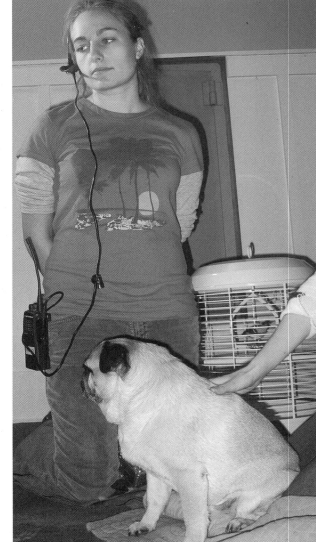

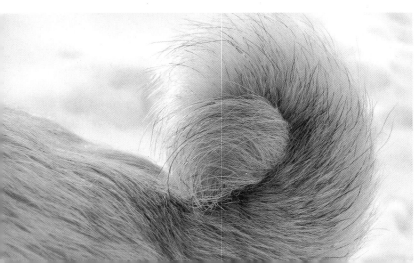

Present at the medium's table that night were Winnipeg's most respected city fathers, including the incorruptible Mayor Cornish, and the madams or shop stewards of our illustrious brothel collectives.
Women respected for their political acumen and clout in the community.
Countless streets in our core area are now named for these great women.

One last time through January.
Coldest, darkest month,
deepest part of the winter.
No end in sight.
The condoms come off.
These are the bareback months of Winnipeg.
Your breath freezes in front of your face
and falls to your feet with a tinkle.
Man and dog, we walk the streets.
Spanky, my guide dog through time.

Even people who have never
encountered snow
can imagine what it's like to walk through it.
You leave footprints, declivities.
When you step on fresh snow
you pack it down.
You pack it down onto the sidewalk and
when all the loose snow later blows away,
it leaves a positive record of that negative space.

Isabella Rossellini told me she once had a pet pig named Spanky. It was wonderfully smart but unfortunately grew to be the size of couch. Every night, while Isabella slept, Spanky would rise from bed, go downstairs and rape all the furniture in her home. By morning every room had been completely rearranged and Spanky could be found spent and snoring in the midst of the carnage.

My girlfriend's dog, Spanky, was easily my best friend during the lonely weeks spent planning this movie. Four times a day I would take him for a long snowy walk to daydream about my city, my place within it and my place within time. I liked to let Spanky lead, off leash, and he appreciated this, occasionally checking over his shoulder to make sure with a nod I was still following him on his tour of the streets. Back and forth across our neighbourhoods we strolled, and my reveries inevitably took on the melancholic aspect such long walks always produce, always tipping me into that graveyard spiral. It was because of Spanky that I was put in mind of the great literature of walking, of Rousseau, Walser and Sebald, and I knew that *MW* would have to be a 'walking film,' a movie aspiring to be made in the spirit of those long literary rambles, no matter how important its train-car conceits might be. O, Spanky, dearest friend, closest collaborator and great canine *flâneur*, wherever you are walking now, I shall always love and miss you, and henceforth always mark out the passage of time in those footstep units we laid out those years together, while we dreamt of this city.

One Saturday, while I'm playing at Tom Laluk's family beauty salon – yes, my best friend also grew up in a beauty salon – my grandmother retrieves from between our front doors, for those of us who can see, the big fat weekend edition of the *Winnipeg Free Press*. Somehow, my grandmother allows all the sections to slide from her grasp, to spill, as bad luck would have it, all the way down our basement stairs. Grandmother lurches to catch all the news, loses her balance and falls after the papers, down those same deadly stairs, down the same stairs up which, in my earliest childhood memory, my father lifted me because I couldn't climb them myself; she falls down the stairs beneath which my aunt Lil's hairdressing employees slinkily change into their uniforms and eat their lunches, the stairs beside which we store all our Christmas decorations and the big trunk of Halloween costumes we dive into every fall. The stairs of an aspiring death chamber. Grandma finally completes her basement plummet and lands with a soft thump next to the family Coke machine, unfolding her gentle self way down there in a welter of blood-soaked newspaper – black and white and red all over.

Miraculously, she is unhurt, except for the gaudy gash on her forehead. She is rushed to the hospital and left in the waiting room for hours. Now, the Winnipeg waiting room is an almost holy locus of ancient custom. Even more so than the anterooms of other cities, ours requires its chilled pilgrims to spend a very sacred amount of time, great heaps of time, within its sanctified confines before he or she is acknowledged by any presiding authority. In this traditional place of long lingering, my grandmother, as ordained by ancient ritual, contracts the customary pneumonia. Here in Winnipeg, where we cover the feet of our traffic cops with hay to keep off the winter chill, my grandmother is given, according to dictates, no hay at the hospital. As it was in times of old, so shall it be now, and again.

It leaves your footstep as a little
relief record of itself.
I like to think of these things as snow fossils.
They don't last 600 million years,
they only last a few months.
But you can actually trace through these
snow fossils your own passage up and down
your sidewalk over the course of a winter.
It's a way of walking backward and forward
in winter's time.

Winnipeg,
we negotiate the great white ways.
The snow labyrinths.
Mazes of ectoplasm that determine
our paths through our lives here.
We have little or no choice where we go,
where we sleep, what we feel.

A city of palimpsests,
of skins, of skins beneath skins.
How to decode the signs of this city?
Another civic law here: we're not allowed to
destroy old signage – any old signage.
Instead it's kept,
kept forever at the old-signage graveyard.
Dip into the layers of Winnipeg.

The city just four years older
than my grandmother.

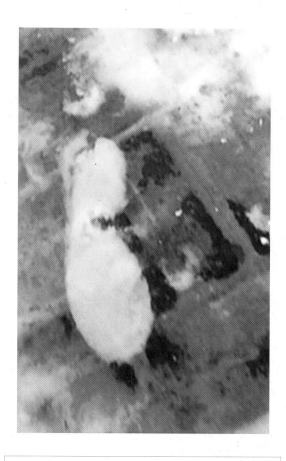

Palimpsests: Winnipeg's first city hall was built
atop the city's third largest river, Brown's Creek,
which in the 1880s was filled in, though unsuc-
cessfully – contractors used too little gravel –
and that first civic edifice fell over just a few
years after construction. Later, with Brown's
Creek filled by both more gravel *and* the ruins of
the first hall, Winnipeg built on this now-secure
site its more famous and long-standing gingerbread city hall, which stood gorgeously on Main
Street until its senseless razing in 1962 to make
way for the current vanilla hall – although something of the newest building's 'block house'
shape appeals to me. There the building sits,
never even suspecting the ghost river that runs
beneath it. May Brown's Creek grow hungry
once more and swallow up this ambivalent
abomination, as is only right and just.

Sometimes so young seeming,
sometimes so ancient.
Frightening.
Frightening is one's place in time.

When the snow starts falling,
the city starts to feel lawless.
Lawless but safe.
All the painted lines on the street are erased
by snow and anything goes.
It's a big game of Bump'em Cars out there.
The lights look pretty.
You can't even see out of your windshield
half the time. You know you can glide
sideways, skidding through a red light,
and the cops will let it go.

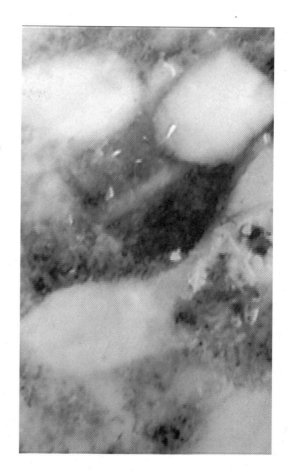

In Winnipeg, it's way more fun for us to
cross the city using only its back lanes.
The city possesses a vast network of these
unofficial streets. A fine grid-like work of
narrow unspoken-of byways
that hold a charm all of their own.
They're not even allowed on city maps,
but the populace knows all about them and
uses them more than the legitimate streets.

A dispute between the city's two main
taxi companies was settled by giving one
company the rights to use the regular streets

In Winnipeg, there are many things with names that would remain anonymous in a less loving city: ditches; school doorways; footbridges; alley intersections; a plank submerged in a creek; certain sewer lids; loose boards in lane fences named after the pursuers once eluded by passing though them; benches; dog holes; gutters; certain high curbs; low curbs; a trash bin that once played an important part in an encounter; yards most easily cut through; the garages most often left open by their owners, piles of oily porn magazines frozen open on the garages' dirt floors; trees named after old school chums they most resemble. All are named, just as streets are! Names for one and all!

Some of the named things. *Above:* Aunt Lil with the Toby Wing Tree, named for the infamous Busby Berkeley casting-couch trophy. *Right:* the Fred and Ginger Tree. *Far right:* the Komidowski Cover, named for my friend Richard, who so loved to inhale the warm air that wafted up year-round from Winnipeg's malodorous netherworld.

while the other company must pick up and
drop off its fares only in the back lanes.
It's inside these black arteries
where the real Winnipeg is found.
Where memories most plausibly come alive.

The network of these lanes suggests
the grid of a secret city laid right on top of
the known one. Lanes with names
remembered only by word of mouth
lie on top of streets named after
politicians and land developers.
The lanes are illicit things best not discussed.
Shameful. They receive the breech ends of
the houses, the side of the home not meant
for the polite company. They are the weedy
landscapes of shameful abandonment,
the conduits of refuse removal.
Here we strew what we no longer want
to acknowledge, and everything,
most notably the Winnipeg Special –
a mattress bent over with fatal stains –
is quickly covered up
by the forgetfulness of our snow.

In the alleyways,
strange wavelengths dominate.
The dispatcher seems to speak directly to you.
The driving is softer, soft as a cushion,
a white pillow plumped.

Handsome Tommy Springman, who taught me
for Grades 5 and 6 at Greenway School, and on
whom I had the worst boy crush ever, retired
early from teaching, took over an old three-car
back-lane cab company called Star Taxi,
changed its name to Spring Taxi and developed
it into a proud fleet that now works the front
streets of Winnipeg.

What is heard in the film here beneath the narration is a tiny sample of the oneiric, torpid hours
of sound sculpture my late brother Cameron
made as a teen with his beloved reel-to-reel tape
recorder and vacuum-tubed radio. He would
slowly dial across all the frequencies available
to us on crystal-clear Kennedy-era nights, layer-
ing one station upon another, and record these
audio strata as they drifted their broadcast opac-
ities on top of sudden and inexplicable clarities.
Cameron's mashed-up recordings were, typically, dreamy and terrifying overlappings of Cold
War newscasts, talk-radio speculations about
Air Force UFO sightings, commercials broadcast live from far-flung furniture stores and car
dealerships in Detroit, Chicago or Houston – the
whole sculpture held together by the tinny staccato beat of all the pop music played in America
during the years leading up to the British invasion, so that, without warning, a bolt of musty
doo-wop could unfurl itself like an immense frat
sweater pulled down over the entire soundscape.

Producer/director of photography Jody Shapiro shooting the Arlington Street Bridge

Then there's the strange case of Lorette.
The hermaphrodite street.
It's half front street, half back lane.
No one speaks of Lorette.

Even the architecture in Winnipeg is sad,
has an addled concept of itself. Emblematic
of this is the Arlington Street Bridge.
A vast span of enfrosted steel girder that
arches over the city's sprawling train yards.
Where trains couple in the fog,
rumble on awhile, then noisily divorce.
The bridge, manufactured some one
hundred years ago by the Vulcan Ironworks
of London, was originally destined for
Egypt, where it was to span the Nile.
But a mistake in specs made the fit with that
river impossible and the bridge was sold at a
bargain price to bargain-crazy Winnipeg.
The bridge has not adjusted well to its
always-strapped foster home.
And it often turns in its sleep while it is
possibly dreaming of its lush and joyous
originally intended home and pops a
girder out of place.

The sounds that groan up from the
train yards at night resemble the agonies
of some colossal arthritis.
Just as the Arlington Street Bridge

Alverstone Street in the West End is another
such transgendered byway.

Then there is Sidewalk City in the Norwood
Flats of Central Winnipeg, which has no front
streets at all, only sidewalks, and all car traffic is
routed down its back lanes – guests arriving by
car must enter the rear end of the house they are
visiting.

In my youth, the Arlington Street Bridge
seemed every bit as doomed as Judy Garland or
Louis Armstrong, two legends who died in
promptly paid installments over the course of
my childhood. In fact, I expected the three
titanic icons to pass from this world synchro-
nously. While Judy staged one overdose or
breakdown after another, and Satchmo stripped
himself of his middle age, his weight, his trum-
pet and finally his kerchief, the bridge at the
end of my street was continually shut down and
laid up beneath a M*A*S*H tent full of workers,
a red ambulance light flashing at its foot. Incredibly, the bridge still carries traffic to this day, four
decades after it buried its tragic contemporaries.

dreams of the Nile,
we have another dreaming, man-made
feature of the skyline.
This one an imposter of the landscape,
Garbage Hill.
The only hill in otherwise
board-flat Winnipeg.
Made from a half-century of the
population's trash, then grassed over and
passed off as a park a generation ago.
This great mound, home to tobogganing
children, dreams its filthy dreams of garbage.
It's not uncommon for kids sliding
down this hill to be impaled on a
rusty piece of rail or old car fender
that's been heaved up by the frost.

My Winnipeg.

A horrific chain reaction of architectural
tragedies started in the late nineties
when our titanic Eaton's department store
on Portage Avenue
hit that prairie iceberg and sank.
Bankruptcy.
Eaton's once dominated this city
to the point where over sixty-five cents of
every Winnipeg shopping dollar was
spent at this single store.
To say it defined Winnipeg retail

My boyhood friend Tommy Laluk was gored by a pair of stag antlers that heaved up from beneath the slope one day – the very antlers tossed in the garbage by his grandfather ten years before my chum was born. If you really want to throw something away in Winnipeg, you have to be very assiduous.

This movie was originally named *Love Me, Love My Winnipeg*, after a civic-pride slogan used here in the 1970s. I loved the imperative ring of that slogan, the take-it-or-leave-it attitude. The threat!

Often, as a hormonally drunken adolescent, I sneaked into the darkened employees' stairwell at Eaton's to climb to its top and peer down into the black shaft that dropped ten storeys beneath me. There I would set fire to my kerosene-soaked GI Joes and plummet them screaming to their deaths, triggering in myself happy lubricities never since surpassed, unless one counts the time – perhaps this was earlier? – when I placed a badminton birdie over myself and urinated into it.

Also razed, and I can barely speak of this, was my beloved Greenway Elementary School, built to last a thousand years. I have just found out that Greenway teacher Miss Louise Staples established, in 1936, the first fully organized, officially recognized city-wide school patrols, or crossing guards, in all of Canada. This team, consisting of fifty Winnipeg pupils divided into five squads, received its Sam Browne belts in a ceremony conducted on the steps of Greenway Elementary School on May 1, 1936. Only now, after stumbling across this piece of history, too late for use in my movie, do I realize the identity of all those white-belted patrols in the archival footage I stumbled across while prepping *My Winnipeg*. Uncannily, these grainy preadolescent phantoms marching out to their posts at nearby intersections were in fact my Greenway school-mates – like me, daily perceivers of that building's interior landscape, its specific echoes and smells, experienced identically but a lifetime ago, and before them the other generations seeing, hearing and smelling the same array that was much later mine in my turn – all of us connected across time by the same sensations! Enchanted school! Like Eaton's and the arena, now blasted to atoms.

would be no exaggeration.

After the bankruptcy, our civic government,

without even trying to dream up an inventive

second life for the old store,

suddenly and unforgivably razed it.

Demolition is one of our city's

few growth industries.

Overnight, construction of a new arena

on the old Eaton's site was announced.

Curiously, after years of public fighting,

with council resisting, refusing to build a

new rink for the NHL Jets, allowing them

to abandon us for Phoenix,

our civic government rushed out this new

architectural lie to Winnipeggers.

The result – a sterile new thrift rink for

minor-league hockey with too few seats to

reach the NHL minimum, should a miracle

ever give us another shot at playing in the

big leagues. A ridiculous, politically

motivated tragedy with the

corporate name MT Centre.

I'm sure memories will accumulate in this

MT Centre, which has nothing but low-

priced newness to recommend it.

Until then, this thoughtless new building

just sits in the windswept downtown corner

like a zombie in a cheap new suit.

Its brick coat somehow meant as an homage

to atomized Eaton's but coming off more as

I once stole from an Eaton's backroom –
although I never think of myself as having klep-
tomania issues – what was certainly the largest
flag ever flown in Winnipeg, at least until the
opening of the first Perkins Restaurant: a
seventy-five-foot Union Jack used to deck out
the storefront during royal visits, post-war
parades and other such colonial celebrations.
It's not like I could wave it around anywhere,
but it had great texture, and many Anglophile
odours that spoke to me of the city's glorious
parade-packed history. I used it in my movie
Tales from the Gimli Hospital as a backdrop,
buried amongst bushes for the film's climactic
musical number, before I returned the massive
bunting to Eaton's for fear of being caught with
a stolen Union Jack, an anti-monarchic crime I
imagined would result in jail time during which
I would be immobilized in concrete and humiliated by the Queen.

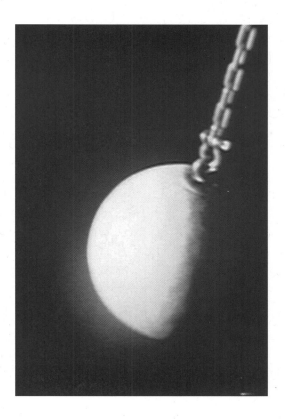

When I'm told that my grandmother has been sent to the hospital, I rush in terror, sheer terror, to visit her, the old old one whom I love so defensively, with a scared, back-pedalling devotion, ever wary of her precarious place in time.

My father is not one for visiting hospitals and has taken himself, the car and his glass eye over to the Winnipeg Arena to watch his team practice. Being fourteen, I have the legs to make my way through the tingly frost to the distant St. Boniface Hospital on foot, past numerous shiny pieces of streetcar track, buried in asphalt since 1955 – when we discontinued streetcars that year, we half-assedly buried rather than tore up all our tracks – now emerging from their past and pushing themselves up through pavement and snow into this heart-sickening time of worry; past the shivering statue of a naked Louis Riel, his posture tortured in response to his genitals being chiselled off earlier that year; along the riverbanks by the Forks where I find numerous strangely warm stones – stones that remember the summer and stay warm well into the winter; past the riverbanks where the Provincial Ski Championships are held every year, each ski run lasting roughly three seconds.

I keep course by reading the great civic olfactory palimpsest: the urine left in snowbanks by the customers of those great Winnipeg lunch counters – Harmon's Drug Store, Picardy's, the Electric Cafe and the Weevil – which all used a lot of canned asparagus in their sandwiches.

I fear for my grandmother.

I think of that strange old photo of her, posed, eyeless as usual, between her adolescent sons, my dad and his older brother – three people, and a total of three eyes among them. An odd double exposure layers upon the head of Uncle Art the shape of the tree that will eventually fall and kill him in a logging accident years later.

I think of that epidemic of deoculations: my childhood friend Richard Nose, who cut out his own peeper while opening a present with a knife on his third birthday; hockey great Fred Dunsmore, his orb torn by a puck; our old boarder Gerry Pinder, his vision halved by the blade of friend Carl Brewer's hockey stick during a vintage WHA contest; Kirk Douglas losing an eye in *The Vikings*, the only film my parents ever watched together – all of these accidents happening long ago, and now too … all at the same time.

I don't notice until I arrive at the hospital's front desk that I have been running all this time with one eye shut. My left cheek has cramped up from the effort this unknowing clench required. I find myself, as cyclopean as my dad, poised at the door of his injurer's room, terrified by what I'll find inside.

an insult to the grand old department store
and an insult to us.

Now the real tragedy.
Since we've suddenly ended up with two
large hockey arenas, the real Winnipeg
arena, the old Winnipeg arena, the most
fabled, myth-and-memory-packed
landmark in our city's history,
has been condemned. Condemned!
In fact, demolition has already begun.
For fifty years, this ice-hockey cathedral
fit Winnipeg and its sport
like a skull fits its brain.
This building was my male parent,
and everything male in my childhood
I picked up right here.

I was even born right here in this
dressing room. Look at it.
Born during a game between the Winnipeg
Maroons and the Trail Smoke Eaters.
I was bundled up and taken straight home
after the game and brought back a few
days later to watch my first complete contest.
My dad worked behind the bench for the
Winnipeg Maroons, the 1964 Allan Cup
winners, senior hockey champs in the days
of the Original Six. And for the Canadian
national team as well, as Winnipeg hosted

Manitoba Hockey Hall of Fame All-Star Teams
In 2000, the Manitoba Hockey Foundation
recognized a century of hockey excellence in
Manitoba, announcing the 'Best.'

1st All-Star Team
   Goal: Terry Sawchuk
   Defence: Babe Pratt, Jack Stewart
   Forwards: Andy Bathgate, Bobby Clarke,
    Bill Mosienko
   Coach: Dick Irvin

2nd All-Star Team
   Goal: Chuck Gardiner
   Defence: Ching Johnson, Ken Reardon
   Forwards: Frank Fredrickson, Bryan
    Hextall, Reg Leach
   Coach: Billy Reay
   Reay has been credited as the first hockey
player to raise his arms and stick in celebration
after scoring a goal. After decades of service to
the Wirtz family, owners of the Black Hawks,
Reay was fired with a note under his office door
shortly before Christmas 1976.

Player of the Century: Terry Sawchuk
Coach of the Century: Dick Irvin
Referee of the Century: Andy Van Hellemond

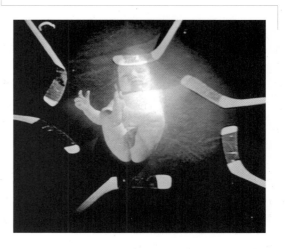

I sat right behind Bobby Hull at this game. He had been scandalously left off the Team Canada roster because he had just signed with the Winnipeg Jets of the upstart World Hockey Association, which rankled petulant Alan Eagleson and the other NHL goons who selected this team. Hull sat with Jets owner Gentle Ben Hatskin in the last row of the reds in the north-end zone.

Ah, the WHA! The sweetest league of them all! If the Winnipeg Maroons were noirish figures lurking in the furry kinescope shadows of my earliest memories, and if my dad's national team burst with Kodachrome saturations onto the centennial splendours of that cinnabar year 1967, then the WHA, a league of hirsute and haggard masturbators, set the dingy and greasy, slothful and profligate, bell-bottomed and brain-dead tenor for the seventies of my teen years, a decade spent listening on Cameron's beloved old radio to Kenny Nicolson and the Jets on the CJOB.

All the WHA teams:
- Alberta Oilers (1972-79, renamed Edmonton Oilers in 1973)
- Chicago Cougars (1972-75)
- Cincinnati Stingers (1975-79)
- Calgary Broncos (never played)/Cleveland Crusaders (1972-76)/ Minnesota Fighting Saints (1976-77)
- Denver Spurs (1975-76)/Ottawa Civics (1976)
- Dayton Aeros (never played)/Houston Aeros (1972-78)
- Indianapolis Racers (1974–78)
- Los Angeles Sharks (1972-74)/Michigan Stags (1974-75)/ Baltimore Blades (1975)
- Minnesota Fighting Saints (1972-76)
- New England Whalers (1972-79)
- New York Raiders (1972-73, renamed New York Golden Blades in 1973)/New Jersey Knights (1973-74)/San Diego Mariners (1974-77)
- Ottawa Nationals (1972-73) / Toronto Toros (1973-76)/ Birmingham Bulls (1976-79)
- Miami Screaming Eagles (never played)/Philadelphia Blazers (1972-73)/Vancouver Blazers (1973-75)/Calgary Cowboys (1975-77)
- Phoenix Roadrunners (1974-77)
- San Francisco Sharks (never played)/Quebec Nordiques (1972-79)
- Winnipeg Jets (1972-79)

wave upon frightening wave of visits from the
revolutionary juggernaut Soviet team,
years before the hubristic NHL deigned to
hold its first summit series in 1972.
Here's my ticket for Game 3 of that series,
a four-all tie. A dull game compared to
the electrifying contests typically held here
at the world capital of international hockey.
The NHL never liked us here in Winnipeg;
they raped us of our best players when
we joined up with them in 1979.

I grew up in the locker rooms, was breastfed
there in the wives' chambers and was often
lent out to visiting teams as a stick boy.

I met my first superstar in the Soviet showers –
I was dazzled by Anatoli Firsov as he
emerged from the steam naked
except for the lather mantling his torso.
Positively smitten by him,
I once stole his famed
number 11 jersey,
taking it home and sliding it over my
nude body to take a few erotically charged
secret slapshots before tossing it into the
Forks for fear the KGB would catch me
wearing it. I nearly fainted from the touch
of its fabric and the fear.

FIRSOV

With one eye cramped shut, I enter my grandmother's hospital room. I have brought some snapshots and a needle with me so she will have something to do in bed. Oddly, dreamily, I've been assured by the nurse at the front desk that my beloved's condition is good and that she'll be coming home tomorrow. But when I see my grandmother, she is clearly not coming home tomorrow. She is weak and disoriented. Her hair is a fright wig. Her false teeth are out – something I've never seen before – collapsing her face around the dark hole of her mouth and compressing her speech into whispered manglings. Her blind gaze is no longer serenely determined but panicked. She shows no interest in the photos I've brought when I slide them into her trembling hands.

While placing the needle between her thumb and forefinger, I notice, stirring in the next bed, a beautiful girl, about the same age as me – fourteen or so. With a great restless heave, the semicomatose girl tosses all her bedding to the floor; her hospital-issue pyjamas have already been shed during her unconscious struggles. She is spread before me – the most beautiful girl I have ever seen, and, since my grandmother is blind, I am able to bulge my eye as much as I like at this writhing roommate, she who is wearing nothing but a bandage on her head and a catheter attached to a bulging bag of amber transparency. I've never seen anything more traumatizingly beautiful in all my life. Purest female nudity, golden catheter tubing, curling curling curling from this golden goddess up into a golden bulging bag – urine of the purest hues! If only I can summon the nerve to approach her bed as I am used to doing with my oblivious grandmother during her nap times, when I bend over close enough to hear her breath to make sure she's alive.

I stare at this blinding newness, forgetting to breathe while vacuuming up nudity teen nudity with my one open eye, a hungry camera eye, until a nurse strides in to pull the curtain across the room, whiting out for this adolescent his dizzying visions.

I check back to my grandma, now grown quiet at my side. She has filled one photo with hundreds of punctures, thousands, until it is ONE BIG FRIGHTENED EYE poked through the photo.

O, Golden Bag of Urine – that first and greatest one –- that to this day films over everything that is beautiful to me, like a sparkling cataract suspending in amber, locking inside this shimmering hardness, together, unchanging despite the passage of decades, both mischievous Time and everything that I love.

Winnipeg Maroons, 1964 Allan Cup champions! Painting by Cris Cleen.

Beloved WHA Jet Veli-Pekka Ketola, iconized. Kenny Nicolson announces from on high.

On off days, I would go to the arena for the strange pleasure I could produce by flipping down every one of the 10,000 seats, admiring them, then flipping them all back up again.

Urine. Breast milk. Sweat.
The hockey cathedral's holy trinity of odours.
These are the smells that will haunt this holy
site forever. No matter what blasphemy
is built here in its stead –
and rest assured it shall be a blasphemy.

When the national team was disbanded by a
federal bureaucrat's stroke of a pen in 1970,
my father died.
With nothing left to do, he died.
I'd like to say he spontaneously combusted
right on the ice of the arena –
that would have been great –
but it was quieter than that.
He shrank into a puff of cigarette smoke,
and was gone.

Now my building lies like a
heart ripped open in the snow,
closed to the public that worshipped in it.

What if Eaton's had never gone down?
What if?

The arena! There, the dark red of the damp armpits of the athletes belonging to the DMCI Maroons, my siblings' indoor track team – sweaty, taut and sexy those colts all. And it was at the arena where, at the end of the notoriously late-running Annual Meet of Champions, they turned the lights out on my brother Cameron, even though he was still high-jumping after all the other competitions had finished.

I never gave it any thought at the time, but after the national hockey team was disbanded, I stumbled across my father in the darkened basement of our house, just the ember of a cigarette visible in the darkness, while he listened to a Berlitz *How to Speak German* record. It never occurred to me until his frequent posthumous return visits in my dreams that he had been planning some sort of flight to another country, but that this escape had been thwarted by poor health.

Collage by Evan Johnson

Black Tuesdays crest

But an odd assortment of players, in their seventies, eighties, nineties and beyond, continues to play in the old barn despite the first few thumps of the wrecker's ball. The team is called the Black Tuesdays in defiance of the day in October of 1929 when the world crashed into depression. The players are old Jets, Maroons or from earlier eras: the Warriors, the Victorias, even the Falcons, who won Canada's first Olympic gold medal in hockey in Antwerp in 1920. Cec Brown, voted athlete of Manitoba's First Century in 1970. Ollie Turnbull. Buster Thornstensen. Curly-headed George Cumbers. Smiley Dzama, so named for the numerous head injuries that have left him eternally happy. Other veteran greats – Baldy Northcott, Fred Dunsmore, the greatest of all the Maroons and best athlete in the history of Manitoba, who as a child lived at three different addresses, all of them on Minto Street. Strangely and perhaps a testament to the mystical synchronicities always holding sway in this city, his future wife, Margaret, dwelt as a child in the same three houses long before meeting her future husband. Billy Mozienko, Winnipegger, scorer of the fastest hat trick in NHL history at twenty-one seconds and owner of a

I've never liked conducting research and my laziness backfired here. I could have sworn the Crash of 1929 happened on a Tuesday, but nope, it happened on Black Thursday.

Fred Dunsmore, the greatest Manitoban athlete of all time.

91

Winnipeg's West-End Women's Swastikas, 1914

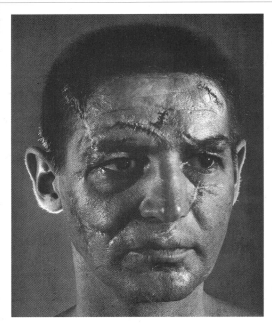

I've always loved the way the hockey stick held by Maroons general manager Terry Hind seems to be beaming from my father's left eye socket directly to Winnipeg.

fantastic bowling alley on north Main.
On the Falcons, Connie Johansson,
Frankie Fredrickson – the most beautiful
of all the Falcons – and Huck Woodman.
It is even rumoured that the heavily
bandaged goaltender who plays is the late
Terry Sawchuk, the NHL's all-time leader
in wins and shutouts at the time of his
mysterious death over three decades ago.
But that's impossible, of course.
They suit up in the collapsing old dressing
room where they laced them up as youths.
No one knows why the Black Tuesdays
formed, they aren't saying. I like to think
they did it to protest the grotesque greed
of the National Hockey League, which made
the sport too rich for this sleepwalking
working-class town.

Game-playing reveries, lost in time.
Mischievous time.
Time flies when you're flying.

The unfeeling coroner's chisel breaks in the
bones at the temples, gets at the memories.
With great sadness, for the last time ever,
and wearing a hard hat, I relieve myself as
I've done a million times before in
the building's famed urinal trough.
The last man in the illustrious history

Enigmatic Winnipegger Terry Sawchuk, the
perpetually tortured soul who tended goal for
the greatest total of NHL victories by the time of
his 1970 death under mysterious circumstances
on Long Island, after reportedly and perhaps
euphemistically 'falling against a barbecue' while
wrestling with Rangers teammate and 'roommate' Ron Stewart, has been honoured in
Winnipeg by having an arena, or more accu-
rately the East Kildonan Incinarena – a strange
double-spirited structure: half skating rink, half
garbage incinerator – named after him. The
Terry Sawchuk Memorial Incinarena hosts the
Manitoba Junior team, the Royal Knights.

I like to think the Black Tuesdays' games are
broadcast by long-dead play-by-play men Kenny
Friar Nicolson and Cactus Jack Wells from my
brother Cam's old pirate radio station, and that
I can receive these signals with the giant radio
I inherited from this ingenious buccaneer sibling
back in 1963.

I met and was spooked by the shade of
Cactus Jack some thirty-three years later in the
basement of a disused ironworks.

It has long been rumoured that Winnipeg's cemeteries have unstable populations that rise and fall from night to night. When the great Winnipeg-born physicist and Manhattan Project martyr Louis B. Slotin was killed in a now-famous 1946 nuclear-fission accident, it was said after his interment at our Shaarey Zedek Cemetery that he had been sealed in a lead-lined coffin to keep radioactivity from contaminating his neighbours. Talk about an unstable population!

Slotin is the subject of *Bloom*, a fantastic book of poems by Montreal's Michael Lista.

Louis Slotin You Will Not Turn Forty

At your fortieth birthday, on a moonlit beach,
One of your guests is late.
You save a plate. A place is clean and set
Amid the after-dinner mess.
Why are you upset? Everyone is here

And laughing wildly, the whole extended gang –
Old friends and family, your little niece,
Your coterie of Nobel laureates, some heads of state,
And Harry's here, and Alvin Graves, their wives,
Their eyes run over with ecstatic tears – even

The palm trees rock with laughter, tossing their hair.
Your forty candles come tickled
To the table, trembling with joy. And your daughter
Laughs from your lap. Japan laughs deep through its ash.
Johanna puts her arms around you and the sky

Spins like a bicycle wheel, the stars
Sliding down their spokes.
But your bomb –
What about your bomb?
It's the only one missing!

We wait well through the night for it to come.

after Ted Hughes

THE FIRE THAT FLIES THROUGH SPACE

I went, just once, in first-year university, to the City Centre on a Friday afternoon, where a bunch of us drank and I saw morbidly obese June Tracy, the grannie stripper who sang music-hall songs while her pendulous breasts swung tassels in both directions and her pet chihuahua Inky jumped back and forth between them in perfect time. It made a lasting impression – when people cheered after each of her songs, she used to say, 'Thank you, relatives.' And after her second or third set, some drunk guy started shouting, 'That's my mom up there!'

Collages by Guy Maddin

of this temple to do so.

Within minutes, the trough will be ripped
into oblivion, and soon too will the great
careers of these wonderful souls.

Kind of a strange victory.
Only the part of the arena added in 1979
to accommodate the arrival of the NHL
in town falls off the structure when the
dynamite goes off.
This I interpret as a sign, a sign that we
never should have joined that league.
I had really hoped this would be some kind
of stay of execution. But no, why did this
happen? Why was this allowed to happen?
The arena, my father, the paternal
amphitheatre of our game, murdered,
all because he lacked luxury boxes.
Here we pride ourselves on the traditions
of labour, and we allow our shrine to be
outraged for its lack of luxury boxes.
I'm ashamed of us.
Ashamed to be a Winnipegger.
Farewell. Farewell, beloved father.

One final experiment for 800 Ellice. It was really
rare for me to side with my mother in family
disputes. I must revisit an incident that puts her
in a sympathetic light to see if it parses out
the same way this time around.

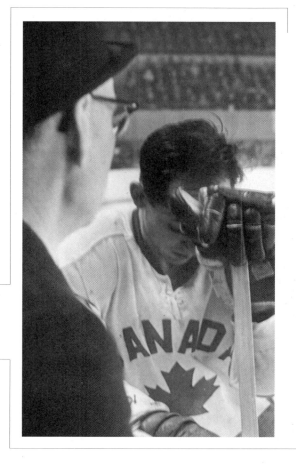

Mother of All Interviews

Herdis Maddin: Pleased to meet you. So you're me, eh? (*laughs*) I love what you do with your hair, so neat and tidy. It's so nice to see someone keeping the hair off the forehead again. I can't stand women these days, with their hair on the forehead. You keep *your* forehead clean, the way it should be. But where I was brought up we were taught to keep the hair off the nape of the neck too. I've never worn my hair long in the back, like you do. That's the only part of the movie I find fault with.

Ann Savage: Thank you, Herdis. I'm delighted you approve! I was concerned you might object to being played by a much younger woman. Columbia Pictures started pulling my hair up in the forties, with those silly pompadours, but I've kept it off the face ever since. What is that scent you are wearing? I can't place it … I'm still loyal to Chanel No. 5, though I think they've ruined it since they stopped ripping the glands out of civet cats. Thank god I still have a supply of No. 5 parfum from the sixties!

HM: I'm wearing Balmain's Vent Vert. My husband, Charlie, brought it back in a golden bottle for me from New York when he played hockey for Frank Sinatra, just after Cameron was born, in 1946, I think. I wear it only on really special occasions. There was never any point in wearing it in the beauty salon with all those hairsprays and perm lotions blowing around by the hair dryers. And I used to put it on whenever Charlie and I went to the movies. We went to see *The Vikings*, with Kirk Douglas, and he took me to *The Poseidon Adventure*. And I went to a hair convention in Chicago. We used to go to a lot of places with the kids before Guy was born.

AS: How lovely on you. Complex. Mysterious. Your Charlie must've loved you very much. Nice to have these wonderful reminders of our men. I keep the No. 5 and Patou's Joy on my dressing table in Baccarat decanters that my Bert bought for me in the 1950s. I wore Bert's velvet robe in the final scene in the snow on *My Winnipeg*, with his handkerchief still in the pocket.

    I never had children, but I have seen plenty of movies! No point in bringing up *The Poseidon Adventure* – it had poor unfortunate Shelley Winters in it, so I *never* saw it. Now Kirk Douglas, what a M-A-N! He used to play tennis at the Beverly Hills Tennis Club with my old friend Gilbert Roland – 'Amigo.' We'd all try to watch them and not get caught. I used to play with Audrey Wilder and Marion Marx – she was married to Zeppo – and sometimes we'd double with Amigo, but never Kirk, unfortunately.

You must be very proud of Guy. I'm sorry I didn't get to meet your other children and grandchildren. I enjoyed working with the actors playing them, and longed to meet your entire family, but there simply wasn't time. Guy has become like a son to me, and fans often ask me if we are actually related – you know, people really believe everything they see in movies – and very often I just say yes he is a wonderful son and I'm very proud of him, and if they press me, I tell them he can be a *tough* director – he kept making me reread those damn lines over and over!

HM: You probably saw more of Guy in two days than I've seen of him in the last ten years. Maybe he *is* your son. He never has time for me anymore. And when he does come over he just falls asleep on the couch. All I need is a light bulb changed and he sleeps. All my babies were good nappers, but Guy's the only one that slept in as a child, and he still sleeps in. I'm terrified to phone him in the mornings. But all that sleeping certainly doesn't hurt his appetite. He cleans me out of my baking as soon as it's out of the oven. I swear, every time we drive by the old bank he used to work at I feel like crying. He's a quitter. But he certainly says lots of nice things about you. You're his favourite! Tell me, Miss Savage, do you ever bake for him?

AS: Ahhhh, ha ha, you have such a funny sense of humour, dear, I see where Guy gets it from. I haven't touched an oven in over forty years. I did take Guy to Canter's Deli in Hollywood for my favourite dish, meatloaf and mashed potatoes – I eat it almost every day - and he sure did wolf it down quick! He's a man with a healthy appetite!

HM: I always have to speak with Guy's friends to find out anything about him and what kind of trouble he's gotten himself into. He never mentioned this Hollywood meatloaf. I suppose he liked it and didn't want to hurt my feelings, or let on how much money he's throwing around. I always had to make *my* meatloaf between customers in the beauty salon. I'd run upstairs and throw a casserole in the oven while a lady dried. But since you don't ever go in a kitchen I'm sure I'm boring you with all this talk.

AS: Not at all. I find it fascinating … I'm beginning to understand Guy so much better. If I'd ever had a son, I would've wanted him to be as smart and kind and talented as Guy.

HM: Do you write all your own dialogue? I swear I never heard a word of talk like this until watching my own life on screen. Guy couldn't even get the dog right.

AS: Oh, Herdis, cut the crap. It's a great game till it's over, and then it's too late!

HM: I guess I should just shut my mouth! And who says it's such a great game? I've just about had it with this world. It's going to hell. You tell me why my son put you in this movie anyway. You seem to know all his secrets.

AS: Honey, you're being about as clear as mud.

HM: Let's just change the subject. (*Long silence.*) I wanted to add that because Kirk Douglas had only one eye, that's why Charlie and he liked each other so much.

AS: What a hunk of a Viking! One of his finest roles! Tell me more about your wonderful Charlie … are he and Guy very alike?

HM: Well, we lost our Charlie when Guy was twenty-one. Guy was so sad. So I've had to raise the boy as a single parent ever since June of 1977. Through all the jobs he's quit, the marriages he's quit,

and that's been tough. Still, Guy tells me I've been a good mother, and that's the sweetest music a woman can hear. And you know, I think I have been a good mother. At ninety-two, just to know Guy needs me, that's all I need. I have no regrets. I'd do everything exactly the same all over again, if I ever get the chance.

AS: Poor Guy, lost his father so young … you know, Herdis, I was raised by a single mother too. I do believe nobody ever loves you as much as your mother. After my Bert died in '69, I moved back to Hollywood to be near my mother. She was so full of love, and after she was gone I regretted every single second that I was snotty to her.

HM: And I know deep down that Guy probably regrets everything he's ever done to me. I always forgive him. And he always comes around. For lunch. Or dinner.

AS: Yes. Guy needs to have someone keep an eye on him. Look after him. If we didn't do it, who would?

HM: I know! I remember one time, he was filming something, and he came down with the flu. He called me and he was crying. He begged me to come over, to take him home and look after him. And he was married then too.

AS: Mother knows best. I'm sure his wife understood, that is, if she knew a damned thing about anything.

HM: Yes! People get so lonely sometimes!

AS: I've never smelled cornbread as sweet as my mother's. She was a farm girl from Mississippi, the only girl in a large family of boys. She loved men. She loved to cook for men and fill their bellies. She wrapped Bert around her finger with one Sunday dinner. A tough New York Jew! What a sucker for southern cooking! Chicken and dumplings. If I'd taken him home for dinner two years earlier, we could've saved ourselves a

lot of trouble, and I would've had two husbands instead of three. I catch a whiff of home cooking and follow it, but it only leads to loneliness. The cold side of the street. Loneliness is my friend. It leads me to books. Movies. New friends. I learn new words. Every day. I learned a new word on Guy's movie. I have a yellow Post-it next to it in my dictionary. *Palimpsest*. Loneliness is a palimpsest. Like Canada, or Winnipeg, or *My Winnipeg*. You are what you love.

HM: I remember when Charlie let Guy ride on Bing Crosby's shoulders. He sure loved that. He was just six years old, and he almost tore Bing's ears off rubbing his thighs on them! We couldn't peel him off! Guy loves so much! So well!

AS: Bing's ears were *big*! Guy must've thought he was riding Dumbo! Sinatra had one *big* ear and one small ear. It was mysterious. Good directors usually have *small* ears, little mouths, big eyes and very big hearts … Edgar Ulmer *loved* people, he was warmhearted … a laugher. When I see his daughter Arianne, she is just like him, she laughs and *loves* people. Edgar didn't tell jokes, there was no time for that, just a real people lover … he understood all the characters in *Detour*. We didn't talk about it, he just knew … and then would quickly shape the performances. Even the least of his movies have respect for the characters, you can feel his empathy, it brings the picture to life. André De Toth and Sam Fuller, same thing. Cukor. George Stevens. Selznick. All wonderful men. But *not* Hitchcock. He was *dull as dirt* – the most awful, boring man I ever met. A mean, fat, lazy fuck. He'd sit there like Buddha and talk down his nose to you. I screwed up *that* audition just so I'd

never have to see that bastard again. Budd Boetticher was another one – cold, cold, cold. He'd prance around Columbia with his riding crop, all the girls thought he was itching to smack us with it. I had so many directors that were cold, efficient, by the book. Those films are tough to watch. Empty. Meeting Guy was a godsend. So kind. So full of love. I waited a long, long time for a good director to show up, and when I saw *Dracula*, I knew Guy was *my* man.

HM: Well, he's *my* man too.

AS: Yes … but he's *my* man *and* … *my* director. And a damned good one. A good director is something more than a man. He's a gentleman, and he knows everything, but keeps his trap shut. He's not a know-it-all. He *knows the score*, and he ain't telling … unless he needs to. You can see it in their movies. Most of the time in Hollywood, an actor is like a pig rooting his snoot through shit, looking for a sweet truffle … and only finding dirt, and poo … *lots* of it! You have to *hang on* to a good director with everything you've got. Listen to him. Hell, I'm ready to marry Guy and start calling you … *Mother*!

JANET

Wake up, Mother. Wake up. You've got to feed us. We're so hungry.

MOTHER

I'm too old to cook anymore. How many times do I have to tell you? There's not a single recipe left in my head.

JANET

Do you want us to starve?

ROSS

We don't know where the pans are.

MOTHER

Make some toast.

JANET

We burned the toast.

CAMERON

Nothing tastes good unless you make it. We throw it all out.

JANET

Or throw it up. It won't stay down.

MOTHER

My kitchen days are over. That's final.

JANET

Whatever you make for yourself, we'll share a little.

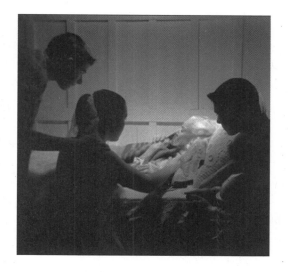

Rejected dialogue:

ROSS

I'm afraid to light the stove.

MOTHER

Open a can of peaches.

ROSS

I cut myself.

MOTHER

Eat some cereal then.

I am so pleased by the power Ann hauled up out of her past and into our little studio in Winnipeg. She didn't reflect light according to the laws of physics – she did that occult, movie-star thing with it, controlling it, amassing it in uncanny ways, mixing it with the silver we still use in our emulsions up here in backward Canada and then radiating with that light from within, and with plenty left over for a pulsing nimbus! And now that she too is gone, how she did all this will always remain a powerful mystery! Simply put, she had it – always did. Somehow, those close-ups of her at the very beginning of the movie loom Rushmore-sized in my mind's eye, but a Rushmore carved from platinum, an image far bigger than any screen could be!

MOTHER

Nothing doing. What's mine is mine.

ROSS

We've brought the parakeet with us.

MOTHER

How dare you!

CAMERON

You were warned.

JANET

We tried to be nice. We tried to reason with you.

ROSS

And you wouldn't listen. Go get her, Muley.

(He removes the top from a standing birdcage. The bird flies out and heads straight for Mother's hair.)

MOTHER

Oh, get him away. Please, God. Get him away from me. He'll wet my hair. He'll peck out my eye.

ALL CHILDREN

Right now.

MOTHER

But I don't remember how.

Rejected dialogue:

CAMERON

You've got a hot plate in here. We can smell it.

MOTHER

What I do or don't do in my room is none of your business.

As a baby, Cameron once cried in his crib for hours and hours. My parents waited him out. It turned out he had an undone safety pin stuck in his skull.

Rejected dialogue:

IN KITCHEN. Mother has a lump of ground beef in a pan that she squeezes with her fingers.

CAMERON

Why do you keep pushing at the meat?

MOTHER

I'm kneading it.

CAMERON

Quit your stalling.

MOTHER

Is the oven turned on? Put it in and let it cook.

JANET

You've got to light the gas. Through that little hole.

MOTHER

Oh, yes. I'd forgotten that.

ROSS

Open a window, somebody. We're going to asphyxiate. You'd like that, wouldn't you? We're on to your tricks.

JANET

You haven't mixed in the ketchup. You think we're blind?

ROSS

And what about the bread crumbs? And the egg?

MOTHER

What do we need an egg for?

ROSS

As if you didn't know. If you were making it for yourself, you'd take the nicest, biggest egg in the carton.

JANET

You're making us do everything.

MOTHER

You know how better than I do.

CAMERON

You want it to taste bad, so we'll leave you alone.

MOTHER

I can barely stand up.

JANET

Get the egg in there.

MOTHER

I'm afraid I'll break it.

JANET

Make a snug little hole in the meat, then stick it in and cover it up.

MOTHER

I feel like such a fool. I'm sorry.

CAMERON

Being sorry won't help a spoiled dinner.

MOTHER

Just a minute here. What's this I see? Nobody's going to get fed until that hall runner gets straightened.

ROSS

That's Dad's job.

MOTHER

Yes, blame the dead for your own carelessness. Well, I won't be able to get up again, but I'm going to make that carpet look presentable. Help me down. Who's going to tug the other end? I'll say this for your father. No one had to ask him twice to get the runner straightened. If we all pitch in we can do this in fifteen minutes. Put that meatloaf down this instant, Janet, or I'll take out the belt, the hairbrush and the waffle iron! Then we'll see who's boss.

JANET

Yes, Mother.

ROSS

Very well. Wet her, Muley. Spray your
filth in her hair.

My mother has always had a strange fear
of birds, I don't know where it came from,
and messy hair too. I remember once we
were down in Warroad, Minnesota,
visiting some friends who had a
seventy-five-year-old myna bird
that had an immense vocabulary and
was allowed to fly free in the house.
It landed on my mother's shoulder
and she smashed it to the floor.
Destroyed, just killed the thing
with one blow. The thing had been living
happily for seventy-five years –
its life was snuffed out just like that.

ROSS

I'll call him off if you get up and make us
some meatloaf.

MOTHER

All right. All right. I'll make you
something.

JANET

Meatloaf.

ALL CHILDREN

Right now!

All my pathological preoccupation with the past, all my nostalgiophilia, all my tireless investigations bent on finding my true place in time's great arc, have yet to find much in the way of approval from the romantic partners in my life, have led me into numerous jackpots situated all too much in the present. By way of illustration, I offer, below, an email recently received.

i read your diaries (*From the Atelier Tovar*, Coach House Books, 2003). at last. you are a piece of shit

my intuition was always right about you – pity my heart fell for you. and you never deserved my heart, my beauty, my uniqueness and my sensitivity. you never deserved my honesty either. you never deserved having such a woman (!) like me in your house, arms and gut. you never deserved all of my effort too. i really went for you – i really thought you and i have been born for each other. but i forgot to notice that i was dealing with a BOY, a 17-year-old springshorts, who just stopped developping.

you never deserved my faithfullness either. you were probably fucking others on the side – DISGUSTING!!!!! I am letting myself be checked at the doctors, for god knows what diseases you carry. you are a disgrace, an abomination that has to be loathed. that has to be isolated.

one day you will feel it ALL - mark my words. but then again you will never understand, and you futile cries of loneliness, pain and despair will go unheard. for you will never understand that it is YOU that creates all of it.

if you think you are done with me – think again. NOONE treates me the way you did, and goes unpunished. i promise you this, Mister Maddin – i will fight till the last drop of my blood. To defend my HONOUR and get back what you stole from me: my HOPES, my DREAMS and my LOVES. my TRUST towards the goodness of mankind. and men.

you are a pathetic hopeless case. no wonder i was having so many vampire dreams after you thrust your disgusting soul into my life. you are a parasite. i want to throw up while even thinking about you – you have filled me up with your dirt, connected me energetically to you and all of your worthless cheap fucks throughout the years. the last word has not been spoken about this.

you do not deserve happiness. i know it now.

and get yourself to a psychiatrist. if you think you can go on fucking young girls, breaking their lives, and do it for 'free' – then think again. and again. men like you should be put on public trial, spit in the face and humiliated.

at least i cost you a LOT of money. I wish i'd even cost you more. and not only broke your heart but also made you bancrupt.

you were right - you are terribly boring. and the reason i enjoyed any of our sex, was because i took charge. you couldn't even get it right in that department. and that after ALL of your 'experience'.

no wonder you have to fuck around. for you know you are worthless – in every department of your life. yes, you know it … that's why you have such low self-esteem and need youngsters to feel 'big' again.

a real man never has the need to do something like that.

the final word has not been spoken. perhaps Death will have mercy on you and let you in sooner. and even then – you will never find any peace in your being. and you will be condemned to terrible loneliness for the rest of your soul's existence.

i pity you. i loathe you. and i warn you. on behalf of Mother Nature.

wishing you all the fun with your fake friends and shallow intimacies – i am sure they will leave you feeling fulfilled in the end. and that they all love you. wake up …

never ever try to contact me in any way, also not in energetical ways.

my being is sealed from you, and so are my dreams.

and i am sending all of your inflicted misery back to you and multiplying it, so that it will hit you very hard

you are not worthy of love. or joy.

you don't even exist.

you are a fantasy.

There's another one for the logbook.

Whittier Park, 1926,
early in the winter,
the first horrible snap of cold.
A fire in the paddocks, started when a
squirrel scorched itself on a power cable.
The horses panicked, frightened,
wildly fleeing from the flames.
One last race – for their lives.
Out into that cruel snap of cold,
no other way to escape the flames but to
cross the Red River. Swimming in the
current, swimming, fighting the current.
That current clogging with jagged chunks
of freeze-up. The ice takes on heft.
Deadliness.
Horribly, everything clogs.
Both horse and ice clog together.
An ice-and-horse jam piles and paralyzes.
Locks. Locks each animal in place by its
panicked bulging neck.
By its frenzied head.
The heads stay this way for the whole
winter, five months at the Forks.
Like eleven knights on a vast white
chessboard. A great public spectacle.
We grow used to the sadness,
simply incorporate it into our days.

Collage by Guy Maddin

105

Collage by Guy Maddin

4

Soon the Holly Snowshoe Club
embarks on weekly jaunts out to the
horse heads and holds little jamborees there.
Winter strollers visit the heads frequently,
often on romantic rambles.
Lovers gather to sit among or even
on the frozen heads for picnics or to spoon
beneath the moonlit dome of our city.
The horse heads are always frozen in those
same transports of animal panic,
an abandonment reading unambiguously to
the young lovers of Winnipeg.
The city enjoys a tremendous baby boom the
following autumn.
Humans born of horses. Happiness.

Now, without a racetrack to slake the city's
thirst for betting, Winnipeggers turn to
wagering on unsanctioned, illicit events,
like the Golden Boy pageants held at the
Paddlewheel nightclub, which sits atop the
brand-new Hudson's Bay Department Store
on Portage Avenue, Eaton's little sister
down the street. Man pageants.
The men are beautiful, the betting is heavy.
Otherwise incorruptible Mayor Cornish
ignores our city's bylaws and presides as the
lone judge at these lurid contests.
He picks the Golden Boy.
Makes or loses fortunes for those patrons

Most of the archival footage used in *MW* is from a fantastic twenty-five-minute collection of 16mm home movies shot by the Holly Snowshoe Club in the years leading up to its thirty-fifth anniversary in 1935. These coed sportsmen seemed to embody Prohibition Era good cheer, featuring a boisterous regimen of wintry outdoor minstrel shows, slow-dancing on ice and permafrost potluck cookouts.

Australian director Paul Cox's first job in film, he once told me, was as a props boy. He was commanded to select for some screen time a horse from a bunch at an Australian dog-food factory. He picked a nice white one from among many brown ones; by putting it in the movie – sliding it beneath the famous rear end of Rudolph Nureyev, in fact – he saved it from the canning machine. But after a day under the ballet star in the heat of the Outback, the horse died of dehydration. So Paul was ordered to fetch another horse from the factory. They were all brown, so he was told to have a brown one painted white to keep continuity with the first day's rushes. After a day of shooting, this second horse died of paint suffocation. And so it went every day for thirty-five days: Paul fetching a horse and having it painted, only to have it die as each day wrapped.

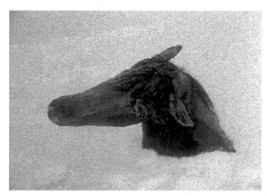

Letter from Louis Negin (*MW*'s Mayor Cornish):

'Darling Guy! How goes it? Was Rotterdam a success? Do let me know. Was at the theatre the other nite, watching Juliette Binoche executing a dance show with a lover – quite uninteresting. In the lobby saw someone who looked like my winner of the Golden Boy beauty contest in 'My Winnipeg' … yes it was him. He's at the National Theatre School here, and was very sweet … no, I did not kiss him. He might be usable for your new film – looks very good and I feel is talented. Small world. Love, Louis.'

in thrall to the vice of gambling.
Trotting, trotting, trotting.
On parade for the mayor.
On parade for Winnipeg.
Thoroughbreds one and all.
Women only in the Crinoline Court
section, please. This is the advent of
modern Winnipeg nightlife.

What does one have to do to be named
the Golden Boy?
What is beauty? Who knows?
That's for the mayor to decide. Desire.
Selecting the lucky one.
The one. The Golden Boy.

The Mayor Cornish era ended in 1940
when scandal erupted over the high number
of Golden Boys holding down golden jobs at
City Hall. These debauched Cornish years
were known as the Orange Jell-O Days,
when the city jiggled to the tempo set by that
simple but timelessly delicious dessert served
in the Paddlewheel as its house specialty.
Jell-O, only orange Jell-O. Night manna
squirting through the teeth into the outer
regions of the mouth and then back into its
centre again. An endless cycle.
The wheel of Jell-O.
The Paddlewheel.

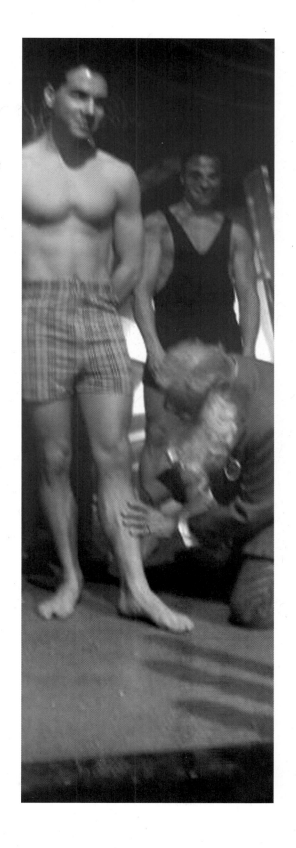

Bijou 498 Main

North — AREAS of COVERAGE

(B) — Arlington St. Bridge   EPIC
    — Winding Sidewalks @ N. Main   STARLAND
    — Former Bordellos
    — Hamilton House
    — Bijou 498 MAIN

— Signage in Exchange | DOWNTOWN CENTRAL | SKATING ON RIVER
— LANES
— Norman Hall 275 Portage Sherbrooke (S of Portage)
— Sherbrooke Pool
— Alhambra Dance 225 Fort   283 Fort   300 Fort of W south of W
— Orpheum Theatre (next to Vendome)   2nd floor
— Victorian Theatre (Vendome on the right)
(4) — Roseland Gardens (Portage + Kennedy S, E, Corner)
— Wpg Theatre (Notre Dame + Adelaide)
— Cave Night Club (Giant Tiger)
(3) — Manitoba Hall (Red Apple)
(4) — Club Morocco
(12) — Dominion 175 Portage EAST
— Silver Slipper Night Club 300-303 Fort
— Mattresses by Gertrude
(5) — The Bay, its crest
(6) — Great West Life for football + hockey
(4) — MTS Centre
— rink @ night
(13) — Nitty Club
(6) — Wpg Clinic   ARTSPACE

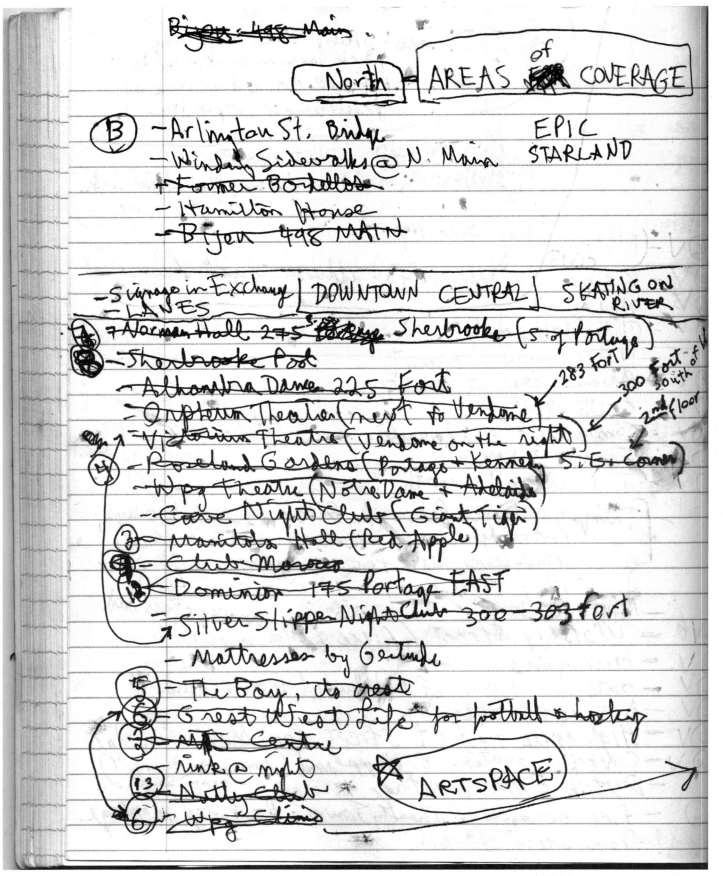

From Guy Maddin's My Winnipeg *notebook*

Betting action at the Paddlewheel, that once-vibrant penthouse of iniquity, drops off rapidly in the decades that follow. Hard to work up much enthusiasm for the pipe-smoking contest held every weekend in the fifties, and by the sixties there was nothing much left but memories of better times.

Nowadays, I fear for the store.
Even sleepwalkers are hard to find here.
One last time, I can still make my way up to the fifth floor, unimpeded by any customers, where the Bay rents out space to the always-nomadic Manitoba Sports Hall of Fame.
There I can find my sister,
and, of course, Fred Dunsmore.
Oh, Fred, why does the Hall of Fame always choose such thin ice upon which to erect its memorial columns?
The Manitoba Sports Hall of Fame has moved many times since I first heard of it.
Every time it moves into a building, the building goes bankrupt. It has to pick up all its photos and banners and sleepwalk to another home.

I worry about the Bay.
Will we always have the Bay blankets?
The blankets worn by my dad's teams,
the famous point blankets that have been

At age ten, by adding what looked like a bonsai Caspar David Friedrich tree, some plaster of Paris and a bag full of hobby-store lichen to the base of the standard-issue plastic Aurora model of the Frankenstein monster, I was able to customize it enough to capture first place in the Paddlewheel's Annual Car Model Contest – Novelty Division.

I won five dollars, which I squandered on milkshakes and Jell-O. The Novelty Division! O, the notional honours of the marginalized category in which I toil to this day, but with camera instead of airplane glue.

The Bay has the best parkade, or multi-level parking lot, in the world – the easiest to enter and exit, and the most available spots, even back in its busiest days. The word *parkade* is used only in Canada, South Africa and Northeastern Pennsylvania.

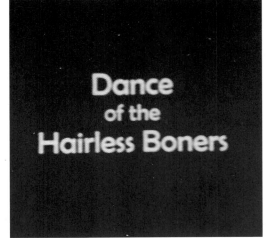

currency for our fur traders since 1670? The city council can't possibly tear this building down. Not again would they dare commit such a murder. Why not? They've killed before and they're unrepentant. But what if they do it again? What if?

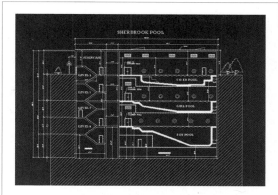

Wake up. You must make one last visit to your beloved Sherbrook Pool, already two-thirds closed. Built in 1931 as a Depression-era make-work project, the facility is actually three swimming pools in one building, but stacked vertically, one atop another. Perhaps the only building of its sort in the world. Segregated by gender, segregated by depths. Families swam on the main level. Street level. One level deeper, it was girls. Girls only. And deeper still, in the deepest of deepest basements, it was the boys. Only boys, in the steamy dankness.

Back in Grade 5, I was invited for a Saturday swim at the baths by my old school chums, only to find upon arriving that my friends had no intention of ever getting into the water. Instead they stripped naked to cavort the day long in the changing rooms. The little savages in their Saturday trances wanted me to strip too, surrounded me, aroused with excitements and threatened to

Sherbrook Pool's deepest level: a maquette.

Collage by Jonah Corne

Producer/director of photography Jody Shapiro, with escorts, in the back of my Volkswagen.

send high arching streams of urine onto me
unless I joined them in their downy caperings.
With engorged little members, hairless.
Why? Why? Why? Why don't we just swim?
While making my way to this boys' level,
the pool beneath the pool beneath the pool,
I always thought of the Forks beneath the
Forks, and a mystical power overtook me.
Something shifted in my chest the
lower I went. A power shift.
It was always rumoured the water in the
boys' pool came directly from the Forks
beneath the Forks. I believe that rumour.
The two lower segregated levels of the pool
are closed now, since 1966.
Why? What if? What if?

If Day! February 19, 1942, at dawn.
Five thousand Nazis invade Winnipeg and
declare martial law. Fascist officers
arrest Mayor Queen, Premier Bracken
and his entire cabinet.
Schoolteachers and politicians alike are
imprisoned in our historic Lower Fort Garry,
which is suddenly a concentration camp
flying the swastika. By mid-morning,
Portage Avenue is already renamed
Hitlerstrasse. Winnipeg itself is renamed
Himmlerstadt. Citizens are bullied,
harassed, molested.

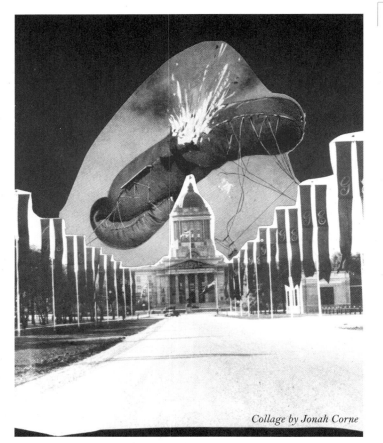

It's very telling, this inability of Winnipeggers to mythologize, or even remember, their history. Considering the similarities between If Day and Orson Welles' *War of the Worlds* radio broadcast – both were faked invasions unleashed upon a gullible public – it's intriguing to compare the vastly different outcomes. The radio broadcast was instantly added to that fat tome of living American folklore, while If Day was never mentioned again in either written or oral history, never passed down to the next generation in misremembered, hyperbolic or boiled-down anecdotes. It was simply experienced and forgotten. Why remember a simulated invasion, Winnipeggers reasoned. Why boast of the event or alter its details, as Americans would? Give us a real invasion and we'll remember that. It took my American friend, the *MW* animator Andy Smetanka, to tell me about If Day, and the American Fox Newsreel Company to supply us with archival footage of the event.

Collage by Jonah Corne

What if?

What if?

What if?

Talk about a terrifying detour through time.

For us here in Winnipeg,

where time cuts many pranks,

this detour is horribly plausible.

The 5,000 Nazis are actually Rotary Club

volunteers wearing costumes rented from

Hollywood, and If Day is a huge success.

Frightening Winnipeggers into colossal

war-bond purchases. To Winnipeggers,

the word *if* is terrifying. In Winnipeg, every

day is If Day. And one must be careful in

changing trains not to take the wrong line.

Not to end up looping back endlessly.

That's why one must stay awake if he actually

wants to get to where he thinks he's going.

To his Happyland – before time or the wrath

of nature in this ancient land plays one more

trick upon him.

Wrathful nature. Quickly, prairie herds

descend upon us again. From the plains of

Silver Heights, the pained cries rising up

from between two mating *pte-wink-pte*,

or homosexual bulls – held to be sacred for

their double spirit by the Ojibwa – spark a

colossal buffalo stampede down into

Happyland. Trampling the playground

There is a great section in British director Michael Powell's *49th Parallel*, his film about a clutch of Nazi spies sneaking across Canada on some nefarious mission, when the sinister invaders pass through Winnipeg, having walked there all the way from Hudson's Bay. They're starving and have no money. They stare, drool bulging their lower lips, into the windows of various Winnipeg eateries, lusting after the piping-hot perogies, cabbage rolls and other vile, delicious Ukrano-*Jüden* treats inside. They visit one tantalizing diner after another, always shut out by penury. It's quite a montage, and I'm dying to know the identity of the restaurants Powell shot. I just have to assume, if the film-maker's team did its research, that one of them was a Salisbury House (founded 1932). So, for *My Winnipeg* I shot a recreation of that mythic Nazi pilgrimage to our greatest institution, the Sals. It didn't make the final cut because of the even-larger Nazi invasion of If Day, but what a film loop this outtake would make: on one side of a large pane of glass, three fiendish Nazis in civvies sleepwalking their way beneath the eaves of the diner's famous little red roof, there to glower, to waver, to quiver their Teutonic lips and double over in the throes of starvation, while on the other side of that pane civilians of Allied nations dipped their chocolate sinkers into steaming cups of the best coffee in the free or fettered world, or gorged themselves on crimson forkfuls of Red Velvet Cake, fortifying them-selves against whatever the enemy could throw at them. No wonder we won the war!

under hoof, leaving it completely flat
within ten minutes.

Then, the third stampede.
This one by our forgotten men,
our veterans of the Great War.
Joined by our First Nations people,
those swelling ranks of our heartsick
dispossessed, these souls descend onto the
devastation of Happyland and sweep up
every last piece of happiness they can, for
they need it. Every fragment of plaything –
roller coaster, arcade, Ferris wheel, every
last sliver of happiness.
They remove it with the swiftness of a
starving man clearing his plate.
These forgotten souls, forgotten families,
forgotten tribes, remove themselves and
these odd spoils to their secret homes upon
the rooftops. To reconstitute as well as they
can from this rubble their own Happyland.
Out of sight, out of mind, invisible –
still there to this day, still there to this day.
Wrathful nature. Benevolent bison.
For Winnipeg has always forbidden the
shantytowns and hobo villages that typically
pop up in other cities. Still on the books here
 is a law that keeps our homeless out of sight
up on the rooftops of our city, above us, an
Aboriginal Happyland.

Collages by Guy Maddin

There was also another large shanty village in Winnipeg, an earthbound one called Rooster Town, a squatter settlement comprised of shacks with no running water, sewer or other services. Many people with modest or low incomes who couldn't afford to live in the city's centre moved out to the edges of the city where land was cheaper. This terrestrial hobo Happy-land was near the Taylor train tracks – great for boxcar-hopping! – on the current site of the Grant Park Shopping Centre, for which the flimsy little squat was razed in the late fifties. According to census polls, there seem to have been no babies born in Rooster Town who grew up to be professionals.

In the clouds, Aboriginal Happyland.
Forgotten Happyland.
Forgotten people, Happyland.
Happyland.

I'm near the edge of town now,
time running out.
I'm really going.
How will Winnipeg be without me?
Who will look after all of its regrets?
I need to think of her as I go.

The *Winnipeg Citizen* was a collective
newspaper that got the workers' word out
during the 1919 strike, the only collective
daily paper in the world. I know the *Citizen*
never had a Page 3 girl, but if it had she
wouldn't just be any tabloid pinup.
She would be … Citizen Girl.
Concerned comrade, sad but strong.
Strong enough to pry herself from the inky
pages and climb to the very top of our city to
tend to those in our aerial Happyland.
And from on high up in Happyland,
straddling our Forks from above,
she could undo all the damage done during
Winnipeg's first trip through time.
With one wave of her hand she could
restore Eaton's, the Jets and the arena.
My old arena home. She would find a

I have an intense fantasy of persuading the long-lived Olivia de Havilland to shoot an extra scene to be tacked onto the end of her 1949 masterpiece, *The Heiress.* I would return to the still-surviving set on the Paramount lot in Hollywood and have her walk back down the very stairs she climbed sixty years ago, then unlock the front door she bolted to keep Monty Clift out, look outside for a second, then climb the stairs and go back to bed. This scene could be shot so simply. I must do it. If I don't do it I shall regret the missed opportunity forever. O, tortures!

The *Citizen* was revived for thirteen months and thirteen days in the 1940s, with immortal Manitoba author Margaret Laurence as one if its editors.

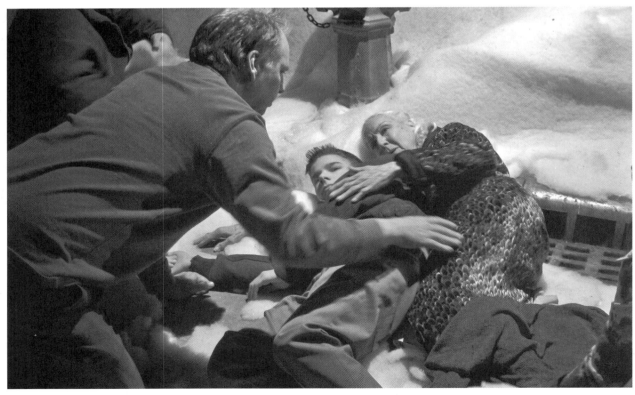

gentle forest for the Black Tuesdays,
those wonderful old souls. She would rename
Minto after Fred Dunsmore.
Reopen all three levels of Sherbrook Pool.
Citizen Girl would plant a new sapling
right in the middle of Wolseley Avenue.
With one wave of the hand, she would refill
the Paddlewheel, raise Whittier Park from
its ashes. Keep all our horses and schoolgirls
safe and right-minded. And once again
turn on the sign at Clifford's.
She would look after this city, my city,
my Winnipeg. She would be its new lap.
And then I would know it was okay to
finally leave. To leave the city in her hands.
Secure. Cared for. Loved.
Then I could go to where there are no ghosts.
Ghosts.
How can one live without his ghosts?
What's a city without its ghosts?
Unknown.
Unknown.
Unknown.

I don't know what this experiment did to my
mother. She really developed an attachment
for my dead brother Cameron,
gone these forty years –
or at least for Brendan, who played him.

Winnipeg street art flourishes even in the window of long-closed Clifford's women's-wear store (now Hakim Optical), where activist stencillers have used the likeness of Nick Hill, legendary Kern-Hill Furniture Co-op huckster, to protest the unremitting doughnut-holing of downtown.

Luce Vigo, the daughter of director Jean Vigo, who died in 1934 when little Luce was just three, once told me she caught a brief glimpse of her father in 1989, fifty-five years after his death, when she screened rushes of *L'Atalante* at the Cinémathèque Française. Luce says she saw her father, and heard him say something like 'Moteur' or 'Be careful, it is going to start.'

I just found an old photo of Aunt Lil — my mother's soft-spoken older sister and boss, the den mother of hive-like Lil's Beauty Shop, all the lithe shop girls who worked there and the throngs of their clients who hobbled into the place seeking the silver helmets it produced for over sixty years. The photo dated from when Lil worked as a chambermaid at the exclusive St. Charles Country Club in 1924. After my aunt's death — at Grace Hospital, by the way — I inherited her diary of that long-ago year and read with amazement of her romantic campaign with a Georgie Urquhart, of how achingly she loved him over the course of the golf season, and how autumn arrived with her, very melodramatically, discovering Georgie kissing another maid out in a shed. My aunt was devastated. So strange to read, so shortly after she died at 85, of the anguished heart-sickness of a young girl, a girl who a half-century later sat with us every night at our dinner table bearing a stout, hard-working commitment to a spinsterhood we never questioned, a state that seemed, to those of us who didn't yet understand the elasticity of time, to stretch way back into forgotten days. But, in the diary, this gentle maiden a-a-a-almost got herself a beau. It was a harrowing read for me, with so much at stake in the suspense concerning the romantic hopes of someone I love as much as possible. Well, twenty years after Lil's death I now suddenly discover Georgie Urquhart himself in a country-club staff photo. Incredible. There he is, bow-tied, predatory, standing behind my aunt (sitting second from the right), a shit-eating grin on his satisfied face. I'd like to wipe that smirk off with sandpaper, except that Georgie Urquhart would be at least 110 years old now.

(Mother lying down with Cameron, holding him.)

MOTHER

It's better between us.

CAMERON

Yes.

MOTHER

Now that you're gone.

CAMERON

I didn't used to like being close.

MOTHER

Why?

CAMERON

I just wasn't comfortable.

MOTHER

Comfortable now?

CAMERON

Mostly. I guess I am.

MOTHER

Me too.

CAMERON *(noticing wrapper stuck to her hair)*

That Freezie wrapper looks sticky.

MOTHER

I don't mind.

My daughter, Jil, gave me the movie's final scene as something she had just dreamed. I was briefly tempted to shoot it with one major change – my mother and brother would still be embracing, but instead of lying on a curb they would be poking out of a hole in river ice, half-submerged in chilled water as if they'd just fallen in, like young Noamie in his snowsuit and the doomed horses of Whittier Park. But I lost my nerve, knowing I'd be pushing the art department over budget, and went with Jil's original dream unchanged.

When Ann Savage's ashes were interred at Hollywood Forever Cemetery in January of 2009, a small party of her closest friends honoured her secular beliefs by blessing her urn with splashes from a bottle of her favourite, Chanel No. 5. A blogger in New York wrote, on the occasion of her passing, 'DETOUR: Femme fatale doesn't even come close to describing what Savage does in this movie. Savage's character would eat a femme fatale for breakfast. And then beat another femme fatale to death with the first one's bones.' Ann has an amazing number of old pals and dead movie folk with her at Holly-wood Forever: Edgar G. Ulmer and his wife, Shirley, with whom Ann was very close in her later years; Harry Cohn; the costume designer Adrian; Marion Davies and Arthur Lake, with whom she acted in *Blondie*; and Bugsy Siegel.

Who's alive? Who is alive?
Who is alive anymore?
So hard to remember, sometimes:
sometimes I forget.
I forget my brother Cameron is gone.
I forget my father has been gone
since I was twenty-one.

At some point,
when you miss a place enough,
the backgrounds in photos become more
important than the people in them.
The old living room where we spent almost
every waking hour lying on couches
in front of the TV set.
My parents and I, lying on couches.
Lying on couches.
Lying on couches.

A chunk of home.
White. Block. House.

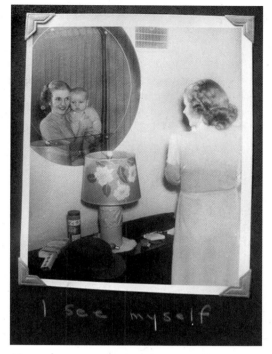

About a year after Cameron left us, an off-duty policeman approached my mother on the Ellice bus, where he said he'd seen her often. He gave her a small assortment of tiny trinkets, photographs and other little mementoes that Cameron had kept with himself to the end. Along with these items, the officer passed along a note no bigger than a business card on which Cameron had written, 'Please let me keep these with me always.'

The man said he'd long felt terrible that the boy's wishes had not been respected.

The city is white as a sheet of paper!

Guy Maddin and Michael Ondaatje:
A Conversation

{Conducted at the Cobourg in Toronto, November 2008}

Michael Ondaatje: Can you place *My Winnipeg* beside any other film that exists, for you, in your memory of film?

Guy Maddin: Films that I've made or just films, period?

MO: Any kind of films. I mean, were you conscious of any role model?

GM: When I first received the commission from the Documentary Channel to make the movie, I was put in mind of a number of things: of travelogues that I used to go to with my aunt Lil as a child – they were delightful, and even as a child I knew they were corny and horrible, but I also loved them unironically. I just loved being with my aunt in a theatre packed full of matrons. And then as a young adult I was aware of those city symphony movies like Berlin's and *Man With a Movie Camera* and a few others, and I'd heard that Atom Egoyan had made one called *Citadel* –

MO: Yeah, it's a wonderful film.

GM: But I still haven't seen it. I've heard that it really loosened him up, made a new Atom out of him, and some really great things came out of it. So I had these things in mind. I also had seen the three-minute Oskar Fischinger movie called *Walking from Munich to Berlin*. In 1927 Fischinger simply packed a 16mm camera, it appears, and took shots of about a second's duration during a long city-to-city walk. It's a wonderful film diary from a period one never associates with film diaries. So all these works went through my mind when I received this assignment from the Documentary Channel. And then I couldn't get Fellini's *I Vitelloni* out of my head, either, because I guess the period of Winnipeg of which I'm the fondest dates from my twenties when I had some *I Vitelloni*–type friends – charismatic but useless guys really wasting their time stylishly – and we used to be able to enchant the city by making rituals out of anything: out of trips to the cheese shop, or to the carwash on Man's Day. There was a carwash that had a Man's Day every Thursday,

so we decided, being men, we would go every Thursday and get our cars washed. One year, International Women's Day coincided with Ladies' Day at the same car wash. We decided to go down to the car wash and try to pick up some girls. We never did, but that wasn't the real point anyway, or so we told ourselves. Stuff like that.

So there were these great rituals I wanted to combine, somehow. And then I realized that from dim memories of *I Vitelloni* – I can't even remember what city the movie's set in, maybe Fellini's hometown, I don't know – but it seemed to be somehow the Winnipeg of Italy. That these guys a little past their 'best before' dates could walk around and enchant the city at night just through the pleasure of each other's company. And the strange weaknesses they each had would somehow form this polymer of enchantments for themselves. They could always at least cast spells on each other if on no one else.

Having thought of all these various things, I knew I couldn't just put them all in a blender and make the movie. I was living with my girlfriend at the time, and we had a dog, Spanky, that I would take for walks – there's something about walking that's better than driving, better than sitting in front of a word processor, even, for digging up ideas. And during these innumerable frosty dog walks, my thoughts always become somewhat melancholic; they always become backward glancing. And I realized while walking – I guess the walking put me in mind of Sebald – and I realized that that was maybe my best bet. I could never be the artist Sebald was, but maybe to make a

movie that, even though there's very little walking in it, is at heart a walking reverie …

MO: Well, your film has a lot of walking in it.

GM: Yes, there is some – and sleepwalking and dog walking. I ended up adding a train element later because I've always loved trains and they enchant as well. I keep using the word *enchant* because, to go back to the moment I was commissioned to make the project, when Michael Burns assigned the project to me he said, 'And don't show me the frozen hellhole everyone knows Winnipeg is. Enchant me. Enchant me.' So it was to be kind of a propaganda piece right from the beginning. But he'd been to Winnipeg only twice and he'd been enchanted both times. Once was to ride, as the sole passenger working as a production assistant, the train used in Terrence Malick's *Days of Heaven* from Winnipeg to Alberta, and the other time was to visit the set of my collaboration with Isabella Rossellini, *My Dad Is 100 Years Old*. For this latter visit he just dropped in on this blasted-out, very postwar-Italian-looking dark movie theatre where we were shooting – an unheated movie theatre – and I think Isabella went over to him for maybe just twenty minutes and poured Italianate warm whispers into his ear for a while, and enchanted him of course, and then he had to catch a plane out of town after this

briefest of visits. So he was enchanted both times – who wouldn't be after such charming samples? It was he who charged me with the job of enchanting the viewer, or attempting to. And then it was Sebald who pushed me out the door and said, 'Think of this as a walking adventure …'

MO: This is with his book *The Rings of Saturn* …

GM: Yes, with the structure a walking book suggests, you can have digressions upon digressions and always still be going somewhere.

MO: There's also something in Sebald's book – he doesn't really say that he's having a breakdown or had a breakdown just before this, but eventually you realize everything he's talking about reflects a state of mind.

GM: Yes. I didn't know if I could pull off something like that, but I thought I would try to discover if I'd had a breakdown that I'd forgotten about, amnesiac that I am. I really have to stress that Sebald was just an inspiration and I certainly don't fancy myself even a shadow of his shadow.

MO: No, but I think it's interesting how one art form reflects another. I know when I was writing *Running in the Family*, about my family in Sri Lanka, it was Paul Thompson's *The Farm Show* that influenced me in that way – the two works are completely different – but he too went back to his hometown and then made a play out of that place – the way you read Sebald and recognized a form.

GM: A form that I was incapable of copying.

MO: Yeah, which is actually great, because you know, because you are incapable of copying it or writing the formal novel, you write this informal novel, which is really your own voice.

GM: Yes, I can brazenly proceed to copy it, knowing I'll fail …

MO: And no one will recognize it.

GM: Exactly. So it was just somehow the pace, the measure, the tone, the flavour – everything is just so pleasing in Sebald that it just gave me enough confidence. But I realized that I'd always started my movies as plagiarisms – I think my very first feature, *Tales from the Gimli Hospital*, I was actually a little bit scared that someone would bust me for copying Erich von Stroheim's *Greed*. And yet when the movie came out, it didn't resemble its source even a little bit. But I thought I was making *Greed*. As a matter of fact, I was originally going to call the movie *Pestilence* just because I liked the one-word title, then I really thought, 'Oh, I'd better not call it *Pestilence* because someone will really know I'm ripping off *Greed*.'

Archangel

MO: There's a line you have in the script: 'What if I film my way out of here?' Is that one of the purposes of art for you? To film your way out of something? I'm not saying that's the only one obviously, but is it one of them?

GM: Well, it never had been, but lately, with the last few projects, I've just tapped into myself more directly, even naming protagonists after myself, as I did in *Brand upon the Brain!* and *Cowards Bend the Knee*. Here I am even narrating it. I've noticed in the past that if I made a movie about something I was obsessed with, the project cured me of the obsession. As a child I always liked the look and feel of World War I movies, but when I finished *Archangel* I was done with that. After working on it for over a year and then talking about it a bit more, I grew really tired of it. Same with mountain pictures and mountains, period, after I'd made *Careful* – never wanted to see a mountain again once I got them out of my system.

And then when I started working on autobiographical things – *Cowards Bend the Knee, Brand upon the Brain!* especially dealt with episodes in my childhood and early adulthood that were mythically big for me. Not traumatic things, but events from those years I loved thinking about. I knew there was the risk in treating these things that if I didn't quite film them correctly there was never going to be another chance, because by the time I was finished the projects I'd be tired of these reminiscences. And that is what happened.

Shooting Careful

You do cure yourself by filming autobiography; it's a weird kind of therapy – you literally just wear out the subject matter. I don't think you surgically arrive at problems that might be troubling you. You don't unearth them, bring them to light, study them, break them down and deal with them or anything like that. What you do when you're making a film about these things is you turn them into words and then into film, you turn them into units of editing, of footage that has to be dealt with. And then you've got to do all that hard work, sometimes tedious stuff: contract signings, sound mixes, colour timings, screenings, receptions and interviews, and by that time you have filmed your way out of your childhood and through your old relationship problems. You actually haven't learned anything – you've just bored yourself talking about them so much. And I was hoping, in a way, that I could film my way out of Winnipeg by either infuriating Winnipeggers so much that living there would become impossible or that I would actually just bore myself with the city by making the picture.

MO: Well, something happens, I think, when you are obsessed with something and then you are shaping it as something out there. You're objectifying it and then the form takes over and deals with it in a more objective way.

GM: Yes, no matter how honest and true you're trying to be about yourself, you're still dealing with a third person somehow, that's shaping that Guy Maddin or that work. I'm sure that must happen with you all the time.

MO: It's strange because you're so intensely involved with the thing and then the form can come in and govern the story …

GM: You're not Michael or Guy anymore – you're a reader or viewer and you just have to worry about the forms.

MO: What was also wonderful about *My Winnipeg* is that, as you have said, all the travelogues we usually see are about Berlin or New York or Istanbul. That's the traditional cityscape for a film, but it's not Winnipeg. So the decision to film it as if this were the centre of the universe was great.

GM: It had always been my goal. You asked right off the bat if there was anything like this in the world. You know what? While making it, I had a funny feeling that I was doing it at a time in film history when other people might be making something similar. It just felt like – I could just feel it – it's not like I see as many films as you might think, travelling the film festivals as much as I do (the fact is, I hardly get to see movies at any of these film festivals). But I could just feel in the air that at this point in film history the boundaries of documentaries are spreading like pancake batter. And it did feel like a logical step to start adding elements of fantasia to the objective. Similar things had been done in literature eons ago; it's a comfort to know film is always behind writing, that film always comes last to innovations. It's behind music, always behind literature. If you track these art forms you can see where the masses will allow film to go in a few years, or decades. I'm not discussing experimental film when I say these things.

MO: I am curious to see Terence Davies' new film about Liverpool, *Of Time and the City*.

GM: It was a real delight for me to see the title of my movie up on marquees in New York, Berlin or Sydney, just as a Winnipegger – as a humble Winnipegger (we're not so humble in Winnipeg). Because one of the reasons I make movies is just to be mischievous, though I don't even know who I'm being mischievous with – with each film it varies. With *Gimli Hospital*, I think I was just trying to see how much I could mess with my family's Icelando-centric pride, you know, I just wanted to break that down as much as possible. With this, I didn't know if I was being mischievous with Winnipeg or with every part of the world that wasn't Winnipeg. I don't know, but it felt mischievous.

MO: Once you start making the film, you have all this raw footage of Winnipeg, and you have family photographs, and I think at one point you say that looking at a family photograph what becomes really interesting is what's in the background. It's not the central character posing for the camera but the dog sniffing the corner of the sofa. And when I was working on *Running in the Family*, there was a similar kind of inspiration from photographs. They just gave me kind of a theatrical space that I could then put invented characters into. Did those fragments, those technical things like photographs and footage – how much did that govern or even continue to direct the story?

GM: I can't remember how many times I walked the dog thinking about this. It was at least three times a day over a

number of months that, even after I'd finished shooting the movie, I would just think of one more thing I wanted to say. And I'd realized years ago that the longer I'd been away from my childhood home, the more I'd dreamt of it every night – it really does haunt my dreams. Now I receive almost no visits from dead loved ones in my dreams, it's just empty architecture for me every night. These architectural dreams are sweetly melancholic … I'm remembering my real childhood home and I can remember with photographic accuracy the light-switch plate in my bedroom, the inside of my desk drawer and how it was organized, the way the shoes hung in my mother's closet – stuff like that. But when I'm awake, I need photographic confirmation of what the insignificant details of my home were exactly like, and these chanced-upon photos are the closest thing to dream experiences I can get while waking. They really send the haunt into me. I didn't feel I'd covered in my narration properly or poetically enough the feeling of looking at the stuff in the background of photos. And I certainly didn't mean to … I think that comes at a point in the movie when I'm looking at a photograph of my grandmother and, you know, I love her like crazy, so I shouldn't have said the backgrounds are more important than the people in them. But just as important, anyway, that the backgrounds come into the foreground and share all the love you have for the person.

I wish I'd taken more pictures of so-called inconsequential things in my first house. Now I just document everything. I'm going crazy in the other direction: I'm taking pictures of every square millimetre of the places important to me. Well, the first thing I did when I went back into my childhood home at 800 Ellice was go straight to my old bedroom door to see if YUG, the dyslexically inscribed letters of my name scrawled there in 1961, were still there, and then I went straight to my old bathroom to see if there was a little dent in the plaster above the heating grate that, when the light from the window came from a certain angle, made a little wolf – what seemed to me like a wolf shape – it's pure cloud-watching, no one else would see a wolf in it, but I'd been dreaming of that wolf shape sadly for years, lamenting, 'I'll never see that wolf shape again.' So I checked that and it was still there, whereas major changes had been made to the house by its new owner: whole doors had been healed over with Gyproc, new doorways had been carved out of walls, a spiral staircase had been dropped through our old living room floor into my aunt Lil's old rooms, disorienting me horribly. But at least those two things – the YUG and the wolf – are still there. And the new owner assured me that those things would never be changed.

The Grandmother in the Story

MO: You wrote in *Brick* about your interest in the form and technical aspects of early silent film … that whole thing about the wish to remove colour and sound and to focus on the grain and how – I am quoting you here – 'The answer lies in the lonely fact that after so many years of musty desuetude, there are still things that old-school silent film does better

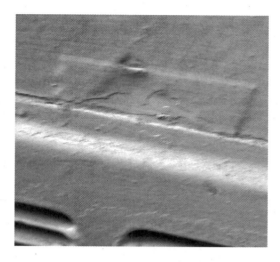

than talkies, and one of these is childhood recollection … [those] narcotically constructed primitive models of the world.' And this has obviously been not just in *My Winnipeg* but in *Brand upon the Brain!* and even earlier films. You have a very – how would I describe it? It's not informal because it's very carefully made – but you are referring to and so seeing through all the technical paraphernalia of film. Thus Louis Negin is given a three-dollar beard in this film. And it is obviously a three-dollar beard!

GM: I know, I often second-guess myself and wonder if I should have gone for the twelve-dollar beard. And I always decide I'm glad he got the three-dollar one.

I think you hear so often among the literal-minded in the film business that it's so important never to break the dramatic illusion, but from a very early age when you're getting bedtime stories from your grandmother, you're both simultaneously in the story and watching your grandmother, and I like to show people the grandmother when I'm making movies. I think people are wrong when they say they don't want the dramatic illusion broken. There's something about silent film that's just a little bit closer to the fairy tale, to the bedtime story, than the talkie is. And I'm just more comfortable thinking of everything as more or less fairy tale and then working my way toward a more accurate assessment of a book, a movie or a story someone's telling me. That's just my

Robert Enright in Cowards Bend the Knee

way in. And then once I get my bearings, I might change my mind about exactly what the story really is. I always like seeing the teller. So when I'm telling I don't mind being seen, or even revealing all my paraphernalia.

MO: I think there's a point in the narration of the film where we actually hear you laughing at something outrageous that you're trying to persuade us about.

GM: Yeah, I wanted to keep that in just because the narration threatens to be pretty one-note, all lugubriousness with an occasional rage fit. I might have been chuckling at how – I honestly can't remember and it wouldn't be in the transcript: '[chuckle]' – but it might have been about how the city council's quite likely to tear down another wonderful building, why not?

By the way, I have no right to complain about the couple of buildings that have been torn down in Winnipeg. I realized when I was narrating this movie live in Berlin that I was talking to people whose entire city had been flattened one generation ago! And If Day doesn't play that well to Berlin audiences either …

MO: Oh, of course.

GM: There can be an un-laughter that goes on with the German audience that's worse than silence. Noah Cowan of the Toronto International Film Festival tried to reassure me that it was the sound of Germans trying to deconstruct things, but it just seemed like an uncomfortable silence to me.

MO: But the thing is, the form you have – we're so used to watching meticulous television or meticulous film – there is something very hypnotic in what you are doing, so that gradually the barriers are broken down between us and the film. We are lost in the streets of Winnipeg. That's what's remarkable. There is a hypnotic and very sophisticated manipulation of us in some way … Added to that is your own voice narrating it.

GM: At first I wasn't at all comfortable with my own voice. Michael Burns insisted that I narrate it. He thought there were so many implausible myths in the movie that if I'd hired a narrator to be me that would just push it over into pure fiction. And so he and my producer, Jody Shapiro, insisted that I narrate it. And I just hated the sound of my own voice. When I write something, I always imagine it being read out loud by James Mason. I really struggled with the command that I must narrate. My friend Robert Enright helped me out by interviewing me in the studio – we all hoped I would forget about the microphone and something natural would come out of my yap, but that only produced so much. Finally, I just went into the recording studio every day for five minutes, telling myself I need not cover anything more than a few sentences. I just started ad libbing, promising myself never to stop talking until I had somehow accidentally said something effective. That's the way the narration was written, slowly, five minutes at a time, over a period of six weeks. I just waded through the shot list, saying whatever came to my head. I'm not a great extemporaneous speaker. Often I just repeated things. Literally the first word that I said, not knowing what I'd say, was just 'Winnipeg.' And then, still not knowing what to say, but promising myself I'd keep on talking, I just said 'Winnipeg' again, and then 'Winnipeg' a third time. And there was something about the third time I said 'Winnipeg' that felt comfortable. All of a sudden I started thinking maybe I should be speaking in a kind of repetitive, railroady, clickety-clack hypnotic way. And so I just made it my goal over the next few days to hypnotize the sound technician, just through repetitions – and there were a lot of

repetitions in my improvisations that were edited out, because if you literally hypnotize the viewer then you've put them to sleep, and that ain't show biz.

MO: In fact, it's odd reading the script, because there are so many repetitions. It is almost like the exaggerated gestures of silent movie in the sentences you have, trying to coax us into something that is really significant, though all it is is three guys sleeping in a train.

GM: I always like those grand gestures that Bruno Schulz, Kafka or Rilke make in their prose where they take something that's so everyday and just inflate it to the point where there's a mythic grandiloquence about it. I don't know … I just felt – I'm a preposterous person – so before anyone calls me on that, I have to make a pre-emptive gesture and make myself obviously preposterous. So I make that melodramatic, grandiloquent move first.

The Hall Runner

MO: Linked to what we were saying earlier on about what is in the background of photographs, I think one of the great scenes in your film is the whole thing about the hall rug being straightened. Suddenly the whole family drama is explained really clearly by this hall runner, where even the dog participates.

GM: I used to think about that hall runner quite a bit. The University of Chicago once engaged me to deliver a lecture and I felt so confident that I could riff on that hall runner for sixty minutes that I put it into the title of my speech. But I ran out of material after about ten minutes and I was really padding for my audience. It still seems like everything in my family comes back to that hall runner. I actually didn't have enough time in the movie to recreate its qualities properly. It had a very gummy, ancient underlay as well. It was my dad and I who adjusted it the most. My father would pull this gummy underlay about two feet toward him and I would be pulling my end two feet toward me and after all our efforts each end would just stretch back to the same place it always was. And then we'd switch to the rug on top, and my dad, who weighed more than I did because I was a kid, would invariably just pull me toward him and I'd fall down and the rug would be more messed up than before we'd started. And I think the family just walking back and forth on it over the next few days would more or less straighten it better than any of our efforts, but with regularity we'd give it a go and mess it up again. So we left everything worse off after each attempt at repair. And sure enough, the duty to repair the runner always called at a moment when I was hyperglycemic and dizzy from eating too many cookies. And then my dad had a heart condition and he was always getting dizzy. And so we were both dizzy and instantly irritated – within seconds – or as soon as we assumed first positions at either end of the runner we'd

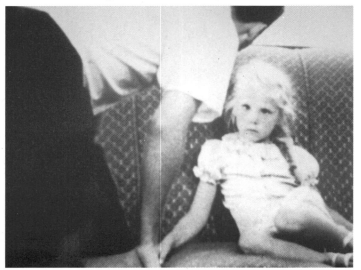

John Harvie with Jilian Maddin in The Dead Father

just pick up at the levels of irritability where we left off last time. And sure enough, dogs and other people would step in, you know, saying, 'What are you doing?' 'Well, you're standing on the rug. We're trying to straighten the rug.' And so it really did seem like nothing else went on in that hallway. I don't remember using the hallway to get from one room to the other. It just seemed to be the locus of irritation.

MO: When I saw your previous film, *Brand upon the Brain!*, it felt like a great forgery. I might have mentioned this to you before, but there's the Borges story where Pierre Menard rewrites *Don Quixote* a century later and it's exactly the same. And the narrator comments that this is a much better version, because it had to somehow deal with the past and also be contemporary. And I really felt *Brand upon the Brain!* was one of these great forgeries of silent film. It had all those elements and yet it was made out of a completely contemporary perspective and contemporary landscapes and cameras and sound (or lack of sound).

Who would be, or what would be, your Don Quixote among filmmakers in the past?

GM: Well, when I first started out it was definitely von Stroheim, but that was more because my friend John Harvie, who was one of my *I Vitelloni* companions, was a kind of 1980s von Stroheim. He just inhabited the past, in ways I've never encountered in anyone else, wherever he went. He toted around a portable gramophone, drove around in a Special Deluxe, flew biplanes. He wore Brilliantine, straw boaters and puttees. On

Friday nights he donned lavender spats, an organdy snood, a honey-coloured corset with a herringbone hem. And always swigged from a hip flask brimming with genuine bathtub gin! There was something instantly enchanting about him, to us boys anyway, and I don't know how he pulled it off. Anyone else tries to do that stuff and it's just goofy, but somehow he pulled it off, and with an arrogant swagger that often got him into dust-ups, great pier-sixers fought to their conclusion in top hat and tails – and he had a way of speaking with the snappy vernacular of pre-Code pictures. Anyway, he turned me on to von Stroheim, always marching about in the director's famous rigid posture. Von Stroheim is really just an erection, after all – shaved close and shiny. And there was just something about the sheer ritual of Harvie, his obsessions with ritual in von Stroheim that, even though the director's stories are quite often nothing special, the attention to detail and ritual just sweep you up with their crazy commitment. I signed up the instant I met Harvie, committed myself to creating movies with him! We really signed a contract, although it was just on a soggy cocktail napkin. But that was at the beginning, when I thought everything was possible.

So I set out, as I confessed earlier, to remake *Greed*. But I didn't have the patience or the megalomania of von Stroheim to pay that kind of attention to detail, and I quickly became my own thing. So I wasn't as successful as Pierre Menard. I was a really sloppy Menard, which destroys the point of being Menard. No sooner did I start living as von Stroheim than I was taking shortcuts and cutting some of the rituals out, even though it was these very rituals I loved.

Yeah, that's a great question, there must be others …

MO: Would Cocteau be one? Would he or Buñuel –

GM: Buñuel is huge for me. Buñuel is so durable for me. I just rewatched *The Exterminating Angel* and *That Obscure Object of Desire* and those movies are even better now than when I first encountered them – and that's obviously the way it should be for great movies. He and von Stroheim were my first two loves. I watched his *L'Age d'Or* as many times as I

Erik Steffen Maahs as Guy in Brand upon the Brain!

watched *Foolish Wives*. We had a 16mm projector and we had prints of those two movies and we would just – when we'd failed in our attempts to drag women to my apartment, a failure that was daily – we'd just stay up all night wearing old clothes plucked from a mildewy steamer trunk and watching *L'Age d'Or* and *Foolish Wives* over and over again.

MO: Even Buñuel's *Wuthering Heights* is fantastic.

GM: Isn't it? It's great because he has that great mausoleum scene in it. That's really wonderful. And I think he cited that as his favourite book, if I recall from his autobiography, *My Last Sigh*. As soon as I read that was his favourite, I read it.

MO: I love that – how someone from Spain loves a book from England –

GM: And then shoots it in Mexico! But it makes as much sense, if not more, in Mexico.

MO: Exactly.

GM: And somehow von Sternberg was also very important to me. Though you almost have to approach viewing him from a different point of the compass, and almost no one does. So people often see his movies as kitsch – well, you don't hear that so much anymore – or some sort of obsessive pathology involving Dietrich. But there's something really smart going on.

MO: What is the point of the compass you look at him from?

GM: I don't know if it's the right one, but I think it is the one he would prefer. I just find it amazing that within the first year of talking pictures he was making these … I'm thinking not necessarily of *Blue Angel*, which everyone knows, but *Morocco, Blonde Venus* and *Dishonored*. These slow studies of – well, there's this strange irony that I can't wrap my head around. There's his insistence on not shooting in real locations – in creating a Shanghai or Morocco of the mind. I guess it's because he aggressively declares, 'This is artificial. This is a tale.' I guess he was writing these really long and elaborate Proustian sentences with a vocabulary of the camera, with unbelievably loaded close-ups of Dietrich's face, allowing her to write these sentences along with him by coming up with the most elaborate facial and body syntaxes. You almost have to go to Italian diva cinema – with its massive inventory of grief and jealousy signifiers acted out from head to toe with more complicated nuances than ballerinas could ever dream up. You almost have to look to this forgotten genre of Italian cinema that spilled over from the nineteenth century for something that equals von Sternberg.

He really knew what he was doing – it's just that no one else knew exactly what he was doing. But I love the idea of a single-minded person working alone and succeeding in spite of the likelihood that he would fail to find anyone who understood him. I like Robert Walser for the same reason – those strange sentences of his, which a lot of people might see as obstacles to pleasure, are the point of reading Walser. And so it's like that with those long visual sentences of von Sternberg, except they don't evoke Walser's flavours as much as d'Annunzio's.

MO: How do you protect that kind of singularity? You yourself are one of the few who has a singular perspective. It must be more difficult now than when you began. Or perhaps it's not.

GM: Well, no one wants to copy me, that's for sure. So I'm safe from that side. I'm often worried that I won't have something to shoot next. That I won't have something I'm compelled to treat.

But then other days I feel like there are a million things to write about. I don't know. I'm not even sure my singularity's a good thing anyway. It's odd working in movies where – maybe it's the same as being a writer, I'm not sure – but the commercial end of it is so discouraging. A lot of times I was told when I first started, 'Geez, you know, you're almost impossible to classify,' you know? 'You're one of a kind,' something of which I was really proud until people started telling me, 'Well, it's really hard to market the movie. If only you made a genre movie. Can't you just make a horror film or a crime film? And then you can still be your singular self, but just make a genre picture. That would help.' I was proud of this singularity, so I stubbornly refused to cede to pressures to go genre. Strangely, I finally made a genre movie – well, I made a horror film, but it was a ballet horror film, *Dracula*. It did far better than I ever expected, and I think it was because people knew exactly what to expect. They knew the story, *Dracula*, and they knew what ballet was (and that usually was enough to keep them away from watching a ballet film), but strangely, more people went to that one than anyone could have expected because it was a genre movie, sort of.

Sleepwatching

MO: Are the filmmakers you really admire the same film-makers you get a great pleasure from? Are they the same?

GM: I've never really made the distinction. I guess there are some I really admire, but … It's hard to watch a movie and forget you're hoping to make another film yourself someday, and so I'm almost always looking at movies for something I can – I'll just use the word *steal*, even though I never successfully steal, but an idea can give me another idea. But some filmmakers are just so good that I could never steal from them, you know – Ernst Lubitsch or Frank

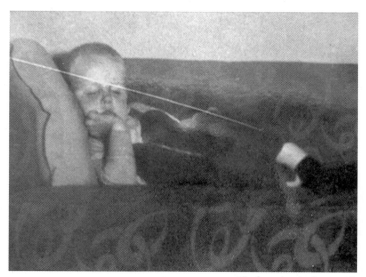

Me, learning to sleepwatch.

Borzage. They're just so good at what they do. And then some contemporary filmmakers I don't even think of stealing from, like Martin Scorsese or Terence Malick, because I just couldn't get past their technical virtuosity. In the case of Lubitsch or Borzage, there is frequently perfection. I could never make a perfect movie. And their gestures are just so elegant – and I'll never be elegant. There's just nothing there for me to lift, so I can just stand back in awe and feel great because such things exist.

And then there are movies that are just horribly flawed and the only reason I'm enjoying watching them is because they seem to be a motherlode of things – of inspiration, of flawed, mad things, of crazy tropes and notions. And I sometimes like reading trashy or second-tier writing – or watching Indonesian exploitation pictures – just for the sheer audacity one can find there. Maybe for the same reason that all the great artists in France in the early twentieth century liked reading *Fantômas* books – you know, even though the writing's not great in those pulps, there's a surfeit of inspired craziness in the pages. So I've found my own *Fantômas* here and there that I like to watch, out in the vast sub-canonical film world. And when I include the sub-canonical films of yesteryear, it often seems I'm picking through all that stuff by myself.

MO: What Lubitsch films do you like?

GM: Well, *The Merry Widow* is perfect. My two favourites might be (I consider them companion pieces because I saw them back-to-back a long time ago) *Trouble in Paradise* and *Design for Living*: these two little romantic triangles. It seems the love triangle is the way to go, because there's so much pain in a triangle – pyrotechnic pain, pain that really spins like those triangular fireworks, fire wheels. It's as if everyone's most propulsive emotions are heading away from one person and toward another, so the triangle really starts spinning. I don't like *Ninotchka* as much as these because there's not a real triangle there. It's just Melvyn Douglas and Greta Garbo. But I love those triangles.

MO: Does a filmmaker like Chris Marker interest you at all?

GM: I do love his film poem/essay, *Sans Soleil*, but I've seen practically nothing else by him.

MO: Really. That's interesting. I thought you would also be drawn to an early one like *La Jetée*.

GM: Ah, that one I've seen too.

MO: It just feels to me like the first film ever made … it must have cost about ninety-five bucks: black-and-white photographs and a French voice-over. And what looks like remnants of old grainy footage.

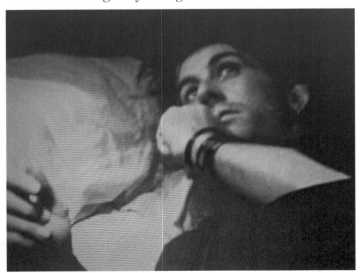

Ben Kasulke in Brand upon the Brain!

GM: Yeah, I know. That's one way to save money on a film: don't use a movie camera. There's the freedom of just, 'Oh, hey, I'm going to make a film out of stills.'

MO: It's only about thirty minutes long, something like that.

GM: And the first time I saw it I was very drowsy, so I didn't enjoy it at all. But I've learned since that first time I saw *Vertigo* and fell asleep – I have to forgive my students for falling asleep during my favourite movies – that sleepiness can be a great omen because *Vertigo* went on to become my favourite movie.

MO: No, I love it when I fall asleep. What's that famous one with angels in Germany?

GM: *Wings of Desire*.

MO: I fall asleep in *Wings of Desire* regularly, a film I love, but I am always awake for the library scene.

GM: I love falling asleep while listening to my favourite music, but it seems blasphemous to fall asleep during a great film – I must do it as much as my students do. But I bet I do it with more affection than my students do.

I've had people tell me they fall asleep during my movies. They come up gleefully to tell me they fall asleep during my movies and they expect me to embrace them gratefully, and they say, 'No, no, I mean that as a compliment.' So I say, 'I'll take it as a compliment then.'

Ballet Lessons

MO: Can you talk about the people you have worked with regularly? I know that you have collaborated with George Toles. Do you have a regular cameraman? Or does it vary?

GM: It does vary, but there's someone special I've been working with lately, on *Brand upon the Brain!* and some recent shorts, named Ben Kasulke. On *My Winnipeg*, Jody Shapiro, my producer, was also the director of photography. I've always liked to pick up a camera myself, and it varies from picture to picture how much I actually shoot. With *Brand upon the Brain!*, Ben and I had two cameras going constantly. I always get first choice of where to place the camera. But I have a very literal-minded way of placing the camera: if I need a shot of someone's face, I just go up and get it. So that leaves Ben all the other choices there are, and so he usually gets way better stuff. I like being greedy and getting first choice. And then, if it's a silent film, I direct while looking through the camera, and the other camera can just keep moving around until it captures something better. Every now and then someone will say, 'Hey, there's a pretty good angle over here,' and I'll just hand them a camera. So we'll have three cameras going at once.

I whisk my Brand upon the Brain! *alter ego, played by Sullivan Brown, off to therapy*

MO: That must be very freeing. You hear about directors getting terrified before the next day's shoot, worrying about the camera angles and movement of the camera. But to allow somebody else to have a second opinion, like a second doctor …

GM: I love it! I guess the last large movie I shot was *The Saddest Music in the World*. I was giving visitors to the set cameras, saying, 'Well, I know how boring movie-making is to watch, so you might as well shoot something and maybe that'll make it more interesting.' And I think we ended up giving camera credits to twelve people.

MO: So if you have two cameras going, is one of you static and the other one moving around? Or you can both move around?

GM: It varies. In *Brand upon the Brain!* there were moments where things were quite frenzied, during the orphans' insurrection, and I would be very thrilled with the footage I was gobbling up with my camera until I realized I had actually had Ben in the frame for the past three minutes. Often Ben and I were filming each other but there were some children caught between us whose performances we were really loving so we never noticed each other. We'd all watch the rushes later and it was really embarrassing because Ben and I would have really long takes of each other in these happy transports of self-absorption with our cameras up to our squinting faces. We would just move around, all over the place, and usually we managed to keep out of the way of the other cameras, and each of us got stuff the other wouldn't think of grabbing. It's something that started when I was shooting the ballet, *Dracula*; I didn't know the ballet at all and there was no way of just reading the script for a ballet. I don't know how to read ballet notation. So Mark Godden, the choreographer, thought the best way for me to learn the choreography would be if I videotaped it from right onstage, in the middle of all the dancers, so he actually held me by the scruff of the neck with the idea that I would be allowed to go wherever I wanted to – but he would quickly grab me out of the way if I was standing exactly where a ballerina with a leg kick could take my head off. And so every now and then he would pull me out of the way. Once among them, I discovered that ballet, when viewed from within its centre, is anything but symmetrical and beautiful. It's really chaotic. You get drenched with sweat when someone does a pirouette. You can hear tutus tearing, panties tearing, tendons tearing, and things go in and out of focus because they're moving away from and toward you in chaotic ways. And with that movie, even though I accepted the assignment very grudgingly and strictly from hunger, I learned the beauty of the extra-sloppiness you get when you can't quite capture everything. And because ballet dancers get tired after just a few takes and you're only allowed to shoot them for six hours a day, and you can't have a Dracula, who's supposed to be omnipotent, flagging while lifting a one-hundred-pound ballerina, I had to shoot it with as many cameras as possible. So that I sort of covered it like a sporting event, but instead of six big video cameras I had six super 8 cameras going at the same time, hiding them behind potted palms and things. That film's editor, Deco Dawson, was the real hero of the quickly nabbed, hand-held shot! He got reams of dynamic stuff. He has been a Ukrainian dancer in Winnipeg's North End, so he wasn't as frightened of the choreography as I was. Bravo, Deco!

So it does vary from project to project, but I do feel so much happier when I get to look through the camera at least some of the time.

MO: And then when you edit, are you always working with one specific editor?

GM: This century I've been working almost exclusively with one editor, a filmmaking partner really, named John Gurdebeke. I feel that he's as much the filmmaker as I am. On *My Winnipeg*, Jody Shapiro was my producer and DOP – he's a documentary filmmaker himself. And that was the first time in my collaboration with Gurdebeke that another editing opinion came in, because John and Jody and I would have these meetings to talk about the overall shape of the movie, because editing a documentary – even though it is a docu-fantasia – is a lot different than editing a narrative film. There are just too many permutations possible. Normally I have the footage mailed directly from the lab to Gurdebeke's house, where he cuts it. And then I just give suggestions or tweak notes over the phone to him after looking at DVDs that he leaves between his back doors – I shouldn't say where he leaves them, someone will find them – but where he leaves DVDs of his

Deco Dawson and Noam Gonick bathe
one another at Atelier Tovar

cutting in a secret hollow tree for me to pick up in the morning. And while he's sleeping during the day, I'm dictating my notes into his answering machine. But quite often there are no notes because he and I developed – or discovered – that we were on exactly the same wavelength when we were cutting *Cowards Bend the Knee*. I know that editors, like writers, need to work alone, to get into that spell, so I was happy to get out of the editing room and just let him do it. I've asked him if he wants to be considered my partner on these films. I've said, 'Do you want "A film by Guy Maddin and John Gurdebeke,"' because I believe that editors are every bit the filmmaker as the director. But he said no, he'd rather be paid.

MO: He didn't fall for that one.

GM: I do welcome the chance to extol the invaluable power of the editor.

MO: So you don't sit down with him and look at the film over a Steenbeck or a digital editing system and go over it scene by scene? It's always through mail or phone calls?

GM: Yup, I haven't set foot in his editing suite since 2002.

MO: This is unusual.

GM: It's pretty unusual. And I remember I used to hold it against filmmakers if they weren't also their own editors because I was my own editor up until then – up until 2002, when Deco cut *Dracula*. And so even to speak of it now I have to swallow a lot of pride and confess that I'm not my own editor, especially since what people like most about the film is the cutting (though a lot of times the cutting irritates people the most too). But I have found an editor I really like. I like to think that I'd be doing something similar, but he's just better than I am. And plus, after you shoot a movie you're exhausted, and I've always had trouble getting the energy back for the long editing process that follows. And quite often the first month of editing was just spent guiltily putting it

off: playing ping-pong or napping or whatever, and just feeling terrible because I was on a schedule and I could never quite get going. So I'm basically just passing on the baton to someone who's fresh at that point.

MO: That's great, I think.

GM: We do get along so nicely, and he does think of things that I could never think of – or it sure feels like I could never think of them. (But you never know what you'd think of until you're actually sitting down to edit.)

And it is the same thing with George Toles. The screenwriter is never a household name. It's always the director that gets attention. Thanks to you – well, in part thanks to you – the public knows Walter Murch. Regular film buffs can name one famous editor, basically, and then maybe a couple of famous screenwriters. Diablo Cody! And that's about it. Screenwriters are so important.

MO: That's a wonderful link between the three of you, because what's great is that it comes to represent one voice. And George Toles, for instance, is very articulate about the power of what he calls in one essay the vertigo of the silent screen; he says, 'The world of silence has the atmosphere of a rollicking graveyard.' It's interesting how the three of you take those principles of silent film and then bring them into the age of sound. I'm so conscious of that – especially in *Brand upon the Brain!* Along with the editing style from another era that goes into this fictional documentary form.

Cowards Bend the Knee

Do you think the process of editing for John Gurdebeke is inspirational or theoretical? He's been given this mass of stuff, and then he has to kind of give it a dramatic form and line, but it's not the usual Hollywood line, it's something crazy.

GM: A lot of times while I'm shooting I'll often be thinking of him because I'm going, 'I wonder what he's going to do with this,' or, 'Here, I'll give him something I know he'll like.' It's almost like I'm lobbing a fat pitch right over the plate to see what he can do with it. And then if he doesn't do it because he's heading in some other direction, then I'll ask him specifically to do that, but that's rare. We're normally in sync. But yeah, he's a good script reader because I never even explain the movie to him. I just give him the script such as it is and the footage, and then he somehow figures it out. I don't know how, because I don't even shoot with slates usually, so there's just stuff — just images coming in with no indication of what to do with them … Now, *My Winnipeg* had some slates for the dialogue scenes, but everything else is just unslated. I think John was a little bit tired for *My Winnipeg* because I had just finished burning him out completely with *Brand upon the*

Brain! (there must be a zillion cuts in that movie), but he really did find — I'm so grateful to him — he really did find the right pace for *Brand upon the Brain!* I had thought while shooting it that it would be really frantically paced. As frantically paced as my previous silent, *Cowards Bend the Knee,* was. But the subject matter of *Cowards Bend the Knee* is more hysterical, it's more mad love and tantrum, Electra-like rage, and *Brand* was a little more reflective. And it's all in the temperature of the temp music you pick to cut to, and so I'd given him all these kind of frantic opera arias to cut to, mad scenes by Maria Callas and things like that. Luckily I'd slipped *Finlandia* by Sibelius in there, but he'd found on that CD all these other cuts by Sibelius that had far more breathing room in them and he cut all the movie to these airy Sibelius pieces – sort of Nordic, chilly, drafty, spacious symphonies. The temp music chosen by Gurdebeke set the temperature for the movie. Having served its purpose, the temp music is then lopped off when you hand the finished cut to the composer to create a new score. So Gurdebeke managed to find that the frantic cutting wasn't fitting the script. He's a really good reader. As I find, as I'm sure you know with Walter Murch, good editors are very good readers. I love hanging with my editor friends – David Wharnsby, Reg Harkema and Deco Dawson, just not in an editing room. I also like talking to directors of photography. There are just certain professional people I almost always like to be with. I've liked every one of my DOPS tremendously. I feel I could be very happy living in a utopian cult of editors, screenwriters, sound designers and DOPS, especially DOPS.

MO: Do you talk to them before you film, or just in general?

GM: I just enjoy discussing stuff – I enjoy the company of cameramen, that's all. They have a way of seeing the world that I cannot find, even though I'm my own cameraman now and then. But I like listening to them talk … There is a great bonus on the Criterion *Days of Heaven* release where they're talking to the camera operator for Néstor Almendros, and just to listen to him talk is so pleasant – he discusses the way light hits something, the effect of the light and the backlighting from the sun … Because that's really watching a movie, when you start thinking of where the light's coming from and what effects it gets. I could never be that kind of photographer, but I can listen to that kind forever.

MO: Well, you are – there's that image of the wolf head you recognized on the wall in your family home. You could have gone in that direction.

GM: It's strange that George Toles wrote the dialogue for what is basically a word-for-word transcription of what happened in my childhood. But George has always written my dialogue. I just can't write dialogue. I like the way his dialogue comes out: he'll add definite articles to make people speak in grammatically correct sentences. And I just love the micron-dial twist toward mannered that he gave my own actual life's transcripts. He just said, 'So what do you want this discussion to be about?' and I told him what my folks said and he wrote it down so it came out in Tolesian phrasings – very pleasing to me. And then Ann Savage gets to deliver the dialogue. It's great to hear your own childhood reconstructed by George. George and I have some similar emotional touchstones, stuff from our childhoods. The deaths of our fathers are similar – strange and equally haunting. And our mothers continue to live forever and will live well beyond the grave for both of us. I think that was why we hit it off the instant we met.

MO: How long have you known him?

GM: I met him about half a lifetime ago. I met him when I was twenty-four. He's eight years older, but I think of him as my father, basically; I met him shortly after my father died. But he's also capable of being unbelievably juvenile, in the ways I need. So sometimes he and I are both children. We're both over fifty now.

MO: He writes great essays too, beautiful essays.

GM: Oh, they're beautiful. He just finished writing an afterword for Henry Green's *Back*. That's a book that matters a lot to me. I love that book and it's been out of print forever, but Dalkey Archive has come out with it.

MO: There's something you have said about looking at the photographs of your parents before you were born, when you were not yet there, and how they looked much more glamorous then. So that you were able to fictionalize them more easily.

GM: It's something Nabokov speaks about, too, in *Speak, Memory* – about the idea of looking at photos of his family that don't include him giving him the chills somehow. I can't remember exactly the effect. But for me it was a little different. I think my parents were exhausted by the first three children, so that when I was brought home from the hospital they just put me down on the floor and left me alone, thank God. I wouldn't have it any other way.

MO: Not on the hall rug, though …

GM: No, not on the hall rug. That would have given me too much commotion. No, I was just left alone. But I think I was somehow put down facing the wrong direction and I think I've always been sort of backward glancing. I was just left alone in the house with this photo album, and everyone petered out in their zeal for taking pictures before I was born. My dad still had hair in these photos and my toys, which were all hand-me-downs, still had their heads, all their parts were in place. And everyone was smiling a lot more in these photos than I was used to – I guess because it was for the sake

of the photograph, but to me it just seemed like everyone was smiling all the time in my prehistory. So I think I've always been drawn to a quality of life that must have existed before my time. And I've always been looking back with a mixture of melancholy and joy – a mixture that I love.

MO: There's so much remarkable, unbelievable content in *My Winnipeg*. One is almost scared to ask how much of this is true. For instance, the Sherbrook pool. The Russian sweater scene …

GM: Well, the Russian sweater is true… well, everything is true, in italics, but that one is literally true. I did – it was with tremendous guilt and fear, because here I had actually stolen Anatoli Firsov's sweater, so perhaps he had nothing to wear that night in the game. And I didn't know what the consequences of that would be, but luckily I never heard a word about it. But also I didn't have the nerve to keep the garment. So it ended up being a senseless crime – I didn't even get anything out of it other than one erection and a lot of terror.

MO: By the end of the film you have the If Day thing, which I assume is real, but by then it feels utterly unbelievable. We have come to the point where we don't believe a thing.

GM: That's the one thing where people are really suspicious. They are going, 'Come on.' But there's actually a Fox newsreel, because Americans are naturally better than Canadians at keeping Canadian myths alive. It took an American, my American animator

Andy Smetanka, who did the animated bison and all that stuff – he's from Missoula, David Lynch's birthtown – he was the one who told me about If Day. He said, 'Of course you must be doing If Day,' and I went, 'What's that?' So it took an American halfway through shooting to tell me about If Day; it was at the last second, and the budget was stretched really tight so we could afford only a few seconds of the Fox newsreel stuff (Fox had sent up some cameramen to Winnipeg to cover If Day). If Day was a tremendous success in Winnipeg, but the same bond-selling campaign was tried in other cities in North America without ever getting off the ground. But in Winnipeg, for some reason, it flew! We could afford only some newsreel stuff, but I wanted to re-enact some of it anyway. We could afford one Nazi officer and two Nazi private uniforms. We put the costumes on some Aryans and went commando – just bolted into the legislative building with these Nazis and filmed them striding about in there! I ran into John Harvard, who's our province's lieutenant-governor, the Queen's representative, while I was sneaking around with these three Nazis and a camera. Harvard was wearing a housecoat and slippers – I thought he would say, 'What's going on – what are you doing with these Nazis?' and all he said was, 'My cablevision's out. I'm going to see if I can get it fixed.' And he went to the security guard at the front to complain about his cablevision and we walked right by the security guards and the lieutenant-governor in his housecoat

and bedroom slippers, and made the shot of the soldiers walking down the front steps inside the legislative building. It was a great moment, the actual shooting. And then we had a book burning outside the legislative building as well without anyone –

MO: Noticing?

GM: Strange what you can do without anyone noticing. It felt really evil. It feels really wrong burning books, anyway; I had to make sure they were calculus textbooks from my old left-hemisphere days. I felt there wouldn't be any loss to world knowledge.

MO: I was talking to the actress Susan Coyne. She's from Winnipeg and she saw the film and said (I told her I was going to talk to you), 'Why no mention of Clifford's department store, where every week they changed the colour of what the mannequins were wearing?'

GM: Yes, I wish I'd had the chance to go further into Clifford's, but I do have a very brief reference to Clifford's at the end, and I planted it there as an in-joke. I tried not to make the movie full of in-jokes for Winnipeggers, but I threw them one when Citizen Girl, at the very end, is raising the arena and planting a sapling to replace the Wolseley Elm – I do have her turning on the neon sign at Clifford's with one wave of the hand. And that's when you can always hear the Winnipeggers in the audience, gasping or giggling a little.

A guy came up to me in Berlin or someplace – I can't remember what city – and bragged that it was his dad who had turned off the Clifford's sign for the last time. But I went, 'No, no, I turned it off for the last time because I actually managed to turn it on one last time for the movie,' and then sadly turned it off.

But talk about therapeutic. I'm saddened by the loss of the Clifford's sign, which was then taken off and replaced with a Hakim Optical sign. As I was really outraged and saddened by the demolition of the arena. At least being there to film part of these deaths made me feel special, and at least I was documenting them. It was a big consolation, not a small one. We had the arena on film in its last days. And I literally did get the last pee in at the men's washroom in the north-end zone there. It was being demolished by a mom-and-pop demolition crew working very slowly from the north end south and I was allowed to go in with a hard hat and my camera with the specific instructions to stay away from the north-end zone and just stick to the south where it was safe. And I just went straight to the north-end zone when I was left alone, and went to the washroom! I remember the urinal troughs where there's always room for one more. Just when you're letting go, someone will come jostling in beside you and let rip and mist you up to your elbows with opera gloves of spritzed urine that you always had to wash – not just your hands but right up to your elbows, and further. And here I was, and there were already thumps just on the other side of the wall from the wrecking ball and little bits of plaster falling. So I went in there, and – talk about trying to produce under pressure – I set the video camera up on a tripod and – I don't like appearing on film, but this is a souvenir I really had to get. And I was able to produce a trickle in front of the camera and right beside the wrecking ball. After I finished shooting I stuck around the site for about another ninety minutes so I could get on videotape the backhoe ripping the washroom to smithereens. It was a way of feeling happy about something unhappy. Everything at that demolition site was so funereal, but this peeing was like sudden laughter at an interment. I felt better about everything because of this pee.

2008 Berlinale catalogue illustration of Spanky

MO: I have a great desire to see the *Ledgeman* films that you invented. I think that is one of the great scenes.

GM: Well, I wish there were some. People always ask, 'Is *Ledgeman* true?' and I always assure them that it is, and that my mother was in them – that the episodes were wedged between a local ventriloquist act and a French-immersion puppet show at lunchtime every day, and that my mother was the sole performer in the role of the mother but that there were five different Ledgemen over the forty-nine and a half years that the show ran. And that there were occasional guest appearances, and that Bobby Hull even appeared on the ledge one day, because the TV station was right next to the arena. Bobby Hull came and stood on the ledge and my mother assured him there was no need to despair, that the Jets just needed a couple of goons on the team to protect the delicate Swedish line mates he had, and things like that. And he came down off the ledge and went out and scored a hat trick that night.

MO: I have one more question, from the actor Louis Negin, who has worked with you often. He said, 'What does his family think?'

GM: I haven't been fair to my family, I have to admit. It was one thing with *Cowards Bend the Knee* to out myself as a scoundrel and a coward, but then with *Brand upon the Brain!*, albeit in a pretty mythically disguised way, I started outing members of my family – certainly nothing malicious. And then with *My Winnipeg* I really went pretty far and started getting people that looked exactly like my siblings and giving them their real names. I guess all I had to do was ask permission of my siblings and mother and they would have given it, I'm sure, but instead I just let them find out by reading reviews … But they've been good about it. And when I tell them I'm planning on making another movie they just say things like, 'Well, what sort of heinous things are you going to do to us next?' So they've been really good about it, actually. I don't know how thrilled they were. My brother's

My cameo in Tales from the Gimli Hospital

been really supportive all through my career, but he did say that the movie hurt a little bit in places. But he didn't grind it in, didn't make me pay at all. And he's proud of me and sweetly sends little clippings about me whenever he finds them.

MO: It's a very generous film, too, I think. It's not a mean film in any way.

GM: No, I sure hope not, and there are some big things that I could have exploited, but maybe I'll save those to exploit for next time. When the trade-off of really hurting loved ones will result in a great profit for me. But in the meantime I'll probably just try to go easy on them.

MO: Just wait for your Hollywood film.

GM: Exactly, out them in HD or something. In the meantime I'll just love them.

Herdis Maddin as the blind grandmother in Cowards Bend the Knee

A Miscellany

{A treasure trove, including colour photographs and art, notebook excerpts
and reflections by Andy Smetanka, Darcy Fehr and Caelum Vatnsdal}

winnipeg

LOS BROVOS MOTOR CYCLE GANG HEADQUARTERS

Kildonan Park THE WITCH'S HUT

The General Strike of 1911

Salisbury House dinner, I worker there for half a year. It is owned by Burton Cummings of (guess who) fame

Rob's House

THE ROYAL ART LODGE

The Royal Art Lodge studio since 1998

Hell's Angels club house

THE BUFFALO DIORAMA IN the Museum of MAN and Nature

The Den of THE GARSOURUS

The Largest Disease centre in North America they test every thing from Anthrax to Bird Flu

THE PLUG IN GALLERY

pee ART

INTO THE MUSIC good VINYL

LEGISLATIVE ALBATROSS

Cinematheque

winnipeg international Airport

LARGE JETS NOW LAND REGULARLY

AIR CANADA

826 Wpg

Sisler High School

THE DZAMA HOUSE HOLD

LEGISLATIVE BUILDING

Garbage hill

WATER TAXI

THE ABANDONED STEEL MILL USED IN GUY MADDIN'S CLASSIC HEART OF THE WORLD and SADDEST MUSIC IN THE WORLD

Neil Youngs High School

ASSINIBOINE PARK

Assiniboia Downs

LIVE thoroughbred racing I once won $400.00 on a Horse NAMED SLUGGER

map

THE FRENCH QUARTER

THE TINKER TOWN TICK

N W E S

• THE ROYAL CANADIAN MINT
where Canadian money is made called LOONIES + TOONIES

• The great MS PADDLEWHEEL DISASTER OF 1984

Exchange DISTRICT

OLD ST BONIFACE

THE GIANT SQUID OF THE RED

Portage and Main -50 Below

THE Forks

THE HUMANE SOCIETY WHERE PIP CAME FROM

Winnipeg Art Gallery

The Highgate HAUNTED

FIRST FAMILY HOME

THE GRAVE OF LOUIS RIEL THE CHARISMATIC MÉTIS LEADER WHO LEAD THE REBELLION ON CANADA

THE GRAVE OF GREAT GRANDPA DZAMA FAMOUS TRAIN ROBBER OF 1888 AND HIS SIDE KICK TED.

RED RIVER

THE PICKERAL FISH OF THE RED

THE BAT CAVE OF FOSSTON HILL

UNIVERSITY OF MANITOBA THE FITZGERAID BUILDING 1st meeting of the Royal Art Lodge 1996

Marcel Dzama

Until 2008, the Winnipeg Zoo held within its bars the world's most elderly polar bear, a forty-three-year-old creature at least twice as aged as the next oldest on the globe. The thing was absolutely demented, pacing back and forth over the same worn-down granite path some fifteen feet long, insanely stir-crazy, manifesting an incredible array of heartbreaking nervous quirks usually seen only in dissertation writers. Adoring kids fed this poor trapped thing pennies and nickels for all its pacing, a reward for the upward wagging of its jaw performed at the end of each completed route on its little path, that rock rut grooved ever more deeply into the floor of its ersatz cave. This grotesque and inexplicable jaw-wagging must have been performed hundreds of millions of times over the years. This late bear – Debbie was her name – enabled Winnipeggers to pay admission to come see themselves for over four decades. Now that she's gone, no one knows how we will replace her, or who could pay us a tribute as loving as hers.

Kitty-corner from 800 Ellice was the Chili Bowl, a great greasy spoon featuring a stuffed giraffe's head mounted on the wall. This poor creature was the first African roadkill in North America when it escaped the Winnipeg Zoo in 1927 and was run down by a Model T Ford on what is now Corydon Avenue. When the Chili Bowl was razed to make way for a 7-Eleven in 1970, I rescued the giraffe from the rubble and have kept it ever since.

Ah, the African animals of Winnipeg! One year, a scheduling snafu led to the Shrine Circus moving its animals into the Winnipeg Arena a night early. The carnies were forced to leave a couple cages of lions in the small space of floor between the stands and the boards of the hockey rink until the end of the Maroons game would allow them more room. I'll never forget the roars and agonized cries of the big cats whenever a stray slapshot from Fred Dunsmore or Ross Parke sent the puck ricocheting into these front-row prisons.

Cramped space was often a charming problem at the arena, and large exotic animals, as a result, were often given the chance to balance accounts with their human captors. My friend Jeff Solylo, who sold popcorn at the circus, tells me the kids refilled their concession trays right next to where the elephants were watered. Whenever an elephant made water in its turn, a tremendous mist of urine wafted over each and every bag of popcorn as the kids were loaded up with the salty treats for delivery to the hungry Winnipeggers packing the stands.

Eaton's Flaming Wrecking Ball, *a collage by Guy Maddin*

Collage by Guy Maddin

The old Basilica, along with the Legislative Building one of greater Winnipeg's two most spectacular constructions, was the architectural, religious and cultural capital of Winnipeg's French-speaking twin city across the Red, St. Boniface. The blaze that destroyed it in 1968, before that community joined us Anglos in ambivalent civic unification, was so so upsetting to that populace, so senselessly destructive of splendour, and of such Biblical enormity, that it has to be counted, by Winnipeg's thriving pyromaniac community anyway, the sexiest blaze in our history.

Guy Maddin on Detour:

What can I say? Almost every marriage gone wrong is somehow contained within this masterpiece's corrosive sixty-seven minutes. Tom Neal puts in a sympathetically wormy turn as the rationalizing Everyinvertibrate; Ann Savage is the most frightening femme fatale in film noir history. She and director Edgar G. Ulmer push push push us chumps, the viewers, deeper and deeper into far-fetched, wishy-washy complicity in a crime against plausibility and nuptial decency — yet every frame of this precipitous plummet into the lowest budgets of Poverty Row filmmaking seems eternally, ruthlessly true!

Top: Guy grabs a few pickup shots of Ann Savage in her Angeles home. He thoroughly enjoyed the first Hollywood shoot of his career. Looking on approvingly from the picture tube is Yul Brenner; Ann had her channel selector welded to Turner Classic Movies. *Bottom*: Ann and screenwriter George Toles on-set in Winnipeg.

The Deoculation of Father, *a collage by Galen Johnson*

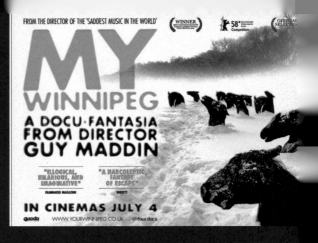

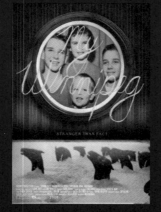

Poster-making is always a painful procedure for directors. We are best left out of all marketing decisions. Nothing ever seems to capture in one sheet of paper the kind of fascination a helmer has for himself and his project, which in my case is the same thing. But I loved all the designs for *My Winnipeg*.

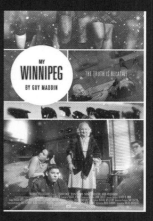

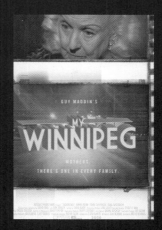

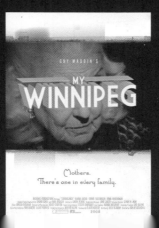

Cold Throbbings: How I Stalked Guy Maddin
by Andy Smetanka, animator of *My Winnipeg*

I've been to Winnipeg once, and not for very long. In fact, if you add up all the time I've spent cutting out silhouette scenes of Winnipeg, it's probably about twice as long as I was actually in Winnipeg.

My friend Sarah and I went there on a pilgrimage. This was in late August 2001, just a few weeks before 9/11. The big news that weekend was a young female R&B singer dying in a plane crash.

It was not as arduous a pilgrimage as we might have encouraged people to believe: I started about five hours away in northern Minnesota, where I was visiting my retired parents, and picked Sarah up in Fargo. We didn't drive the whole half-continent from western Montana like we maybe let on. We said we were from Montana, and plainly there we were in Winnipeg, and we let people draw their own conclusions.

We were there because we were obsessed with the movie *Careful* and we wanted to meet Guy Maddin and his screenwriting partner, George Toles. George had even invited us. His access to Maddin was thrilling to us, and the whole way up Sarah and I giggled and chattered like a couple of schoolgirls.

The closer we got, though, the more nervous we got. Distances seemed to close faster in kilometres, and Sarah and I began soberly discussing strategies for not coming off like complete dorks. We didn't want to be a huge imposition on George and his family, but in our overwhelming enthusiasm we'd practically terrorized him into inviting us, and we didn't see how it wasn't going to be a little awkward once we got there. So we were determined to be charming, inquisitive pilgrims. The last thing we wanted was to feel like George and Guy were just humouring us. You know how that is, that look people get when they're being nice to you but clearly think you're some kind of ticking time bomb. Or just an idiot.

I first learned about *Careful* in an old *Utne Reader* I found in the bathroom of an artists' collective where I used to live. Technically, nobody was supposed to live in this building, called the Atlantic, a turn-of-the-century brick hotel that comes sailing out of an alley in downtown Missoula (population 43,000) like the pirate accounting firm in *The Meaning of Life*. If anyone with a clipboard started asking questions, we Atlantians were under explicit instructions from our landlord to answer that, no, we didn't live there, but that as artists, we needed beds in every room to restore our creativity with frequent naps. Incredibly, this worked for years.

Anyhow, great paper dunes of dumpstered magazines shifted around this place, but for some reason the only thing that ever stuck around in the Sea Monkey–themed third-floor bathroom was a catalogue of sewing notions. Finding fresh reading material was like finding a stack of dollar bills. Leafing through this *Utne Reader*, I chanced on a tiny little capsule review of a movie about alpine villagers obliged to be silent at all times to avoid catastrophic avalanches. I specifically remember the reviewer mentioning honking geese that had to be shot with special silent blunderbusses, and that the print itself looked as though it had been steeped in urine for eighty years. Maybe it was seventy years. Whatever it was, this sure sounded like a movie I needed to see. But instead of going out and finding it, I just sat around dreaming about it for three or four years. I would later learn that Maddin used to do much the same thing before he ever picked up a movie camera, reading about lost silent pictures in library books and remaking them in his imagination. I was in love with the idea of *Careful* the way you fall in love with the idea of a pretty girl who says something nice to you on the last

day of seventh grade before a whole summer of chaste daydreaming.

Part of the lag between reading about *Careful* and actually watching it was pure laziness on my part. Part of it was also fear of letdown and the familiar sinking feeling of a crush turning out to be way better than anything that comes of it. How could the real thing ever measure up to the picture I'd formed in my mind? Also, there was the problem of finding it. No video store in Missoula carried it, and this was before a fellow could just Google his way back to something he vaguely remembered reading about in a bathroom and then order it from Amazon. In any case, it didn't matter. I told everyone I knew about the movie exactly as though I had seen it, confidently rattling off the three or four details I'd gleaned from the *Utne* review: the avalanches and silent rifles and dogs without vocal cords. No one else I knew had even heard of the movie, so the hundred words or so I read in the john made me an authority. It was just the thing to have up my sleeve in the kind of conversation one has so often in one's twenties, sitting around with a bunch of other hipsters trying to one-up each other with obscure film and music recommendations. The pleasure is in the sharing and bonding; no one demands proof. I even acted out the teeth-clacking dogs.

Then one day I overheard the projectionist at the local art house describing a movie to a customer using those same three or four details. Incredibly, here was the one guy I should have asked and had never thought to. Was he talking about *Careful*? I asked, elbowing the other customer to the side. Yeah, he said. Did he have a copy? Sure, he said, he had a screener that got sent to the theatre when the movie came out, and he'd be happy to lend it to me.

He brought the video in the next day and Sarah and I watched it that night, positively stupefied. I can hardly describe what came over me. It was like there was some vestigial lobe or gland in my brain that had been dormant my whole life until this movie came along and squeezed it, and now it was squirting a brand-new endorphin all over the place. I instinctively grasped, too, that the movie was not for everyone, that only select brains could manufacture the special chemical receptor required to appreciate it, which made the experience that much better for its selectivity. By the time the ghost of the swan-feeder father appeared to the mute son the family kept in the attic, I was a stone goner. I couldn't get enough. I started watching *Careful* every day, twice a day sometimes, back-to-back viewings or once in the morning and once in the evening. I clawed people at parties, frantic to tell them about it. I blathered to complete strangers on the bus about it. I talked pretty girls at the bar — there were about five of them, bars I mean, within a literal stone's throw of the commune — into coming up to the collective's hobbit-hole TV room to watch it with me. One of these girls I married.

I got so carried away describing *Careful* to one acquaintance that I completely forgot about the real-life avalanche that had swept

her husband to an icy death only a few months earlier. (In my memory, this mortifying incident unfolds with a sort of Maddinesque flashing of accusatory intertitles: 'Breathtaking tactlessness!' 'Appalling insensitivity!') 'That's okay,' she said, angelically, once I'd finished prying my foot out of my mouth. 'It sounds pretty great.' With not a single rental copy of the movie in town, my obsession became a crusade to get it booked at the art house. The projectionist who loaned me

his copy said he'd been wanting to book *Careful* for years, but his business partner Had always vetoed the idea, claiming it too big a risk. Not for the incest theme, necessarily; she just felt the movie in general might be too 'out there' for her core audience of Woody Allen and Hal Hartley lovers. I could see where she was coming from. As a rule, we Missoulians do not recognize as 'culture' anything that hasn't been extensively profiled on National Public Radio.

Undeterred at the time, I set about trying to change this woman's mind with all the missionary zeal I could muster. I would find an audience for *Careful*, I insisted, make one if I had to, sell Missoula moviegoers a bill of incest and fake mountains if it was the last thing I did. I wheedled for weeks until she finally relented and secured a 16mm print for a one-week run in February – three months away. Worse than waiting for Christmas! When it did open, *Careful* played to packed houses at the New Crystal twice a night for a week. Then another week. Business was so good that the management held it over for a third week. Attendance trickled off a bit, but still up from the usual numbers. A few like-minded weirdos came to see it two or three times; I myself attended every single screening. There were always a few walkouts, and since on most nights I knew literally everyone in the theater, I usually knew who they were and that we could never truly be friends. For the most part, though, polite folk that they are, Missoulians just sat there and took it. I was on tenterhooks for the first eight or ten shows. Any filmmaker can tell you about the perils of watching one's movie in an audience; I was just as keyed up for a movie I had nothing to do with making. My love of *Careful* was and still is completely genuine, but I see now that there was a whole suite of selfish motives behind trying to bring it to Missoula. Part of it, of course, was wanting to bask in a little reflected brilliance: wanting people to recognize Maddin's brilliance and therefore my brilliance for recognizing his brilliance before them. Another part simply needed company: the Montana chapter of the *Careful* Appreciation Society had always pretty much been just Sarah and I, and now Sarah had moved back to Michigan. More than anything, I guess I wanted to write myself into the story somehow. I did kind of walk around thinking it was 'my' movie.

Whatever the admixture of motives, as *Careful*'s self-styled Missoula spokesman and champion, I got the full helping of my fellow citizens' enchantment and disdain afterwards: in about equal measures, and a good deal of it in delayed, time-release nighttime-cold-capsule form. At a very recent art opening, in fact, I was cornered for a full ten minutes by a guy who had seen *Careful* at the Crystal and still remembered every last little thing he hated about it. Had been waiting eight years to tell me, in fact, and not very nicely, either. The great thing was that it was my art opening, at a candle shop, and he was one of six people attending.

The whole sordid affair speaks volumes about this town and my place in it. On the other hand, I still meet people who saw *Careful* at the Crystal and loved it, who break out laughing as they recall their favourite parts and who listen with gratifying interest when I tell them about everything that happened afterwards. The pilgrimage to Winnipeg, for example.

Manitoba is by far the flattest place I've even been. It's so flat you can stand in one place and admire the curvature of the earth in every direction, almost like being on the ocean, only as far away from an actual ocean as it's possible to be in North America. Driving north through this limitless landscape, we found it hard to believe we would eventually run into a city with 600,000 people. Mysterious columns of grey smoke streamed into the sky ahead of us, vanishing as we got closer. The sense of geographic dislocation added to the anticipation, as did our prom-night nerves about what would happen once we got there and called George for directions to his house. We agreed to hold off at first on anecdotes or pronouncements that would reveal the true scary extent of our obsession, however lightly – for example, the fact that I had seen *Careful* over a hundred times. We actually used to play hangman using whole lines from the movie; I once guessed 'Don't forget to wear your sweater at the crevasse' correctly from just 't.' For me, anyway, in all the mounting excitement there was still a small nagging voice telling me to be careful with my expectations. Margaret Atwood, I think, said that loving a book and wanting to meet the author is like loving a pâté and wanting to meet the duck. Practically any obsession is going to be like that.

We had no idea what George Toles looked like, having only seen him under an inch of latex makeup as Count Knotkers' deceased mother. In real life he was lankier than I'd expected, for one thing, waiting between the trees lining the street in front of his house to flag us down, peering over his glasses at us with kind but penetrating eyes. Over cool drinks in his kitchen, we made small talk about the mosquitoes that had started chewing us alive the second we stepped out of the Subaru, and George ran down plans for the evening: dinner out, followed by a water-taxi ride to a riverside concert by the Flatlanders. The following morning: breakfast with Guy. What was I planning to say to the man when I did meet him? I don't remember. I doubt I knew then.

Guy once perfectly described the stupor that comes over you when you meet someone whose fame begs some kind of commemorative interaction, but to whom there's really nothing to say: you stand there 'glassy-eyed and quiver-lipped.' On the eve of meeting my filmmaking idol, I felt poised to relive a disappointing teenage encounter with Metallica drummer Lars Ulrich.

That's why it was awesome to have Sarah along. She took it all in stride. To dispel some of the nerves on the drive up, she concocted endless Would-You-Rather scenarios, forcing me to choose hypothetically between, say, catching a horse fart with my mouth or lying very close to someone we both intensely disliked, for two straight days, kissing and caressing but not permitted to just have sex and get it over with. Having Sarah along was like having my own personal conversation facilitator tossing me softball after softball. I could count on Sarah to subtly pump the bellows of Smetanka inflation. Sharp and funny, it was thanks to her that we were starting to feel less like star-struck dorks and more like real guests.

Halfway through *Careful*'s three-week run at the New Crystal, the *Winnipeg Free Press* – presumably acting on a tip from George Toles – picked up on the juicy news of a Guy Maddin movie riding to the rescue of an insolvent Montana movie theatre. Thus did Winnipeggers learn of Missoula for the first time within weeks of Missoulians first learning of Winnipeg, a historic event that ultimately garnered half a page in Caelum Vatnsdal's delightful *Kino Delirium: The Films of Guy Maddin*, which I submit here in part:

> The local film enthusiast responsible for bringing the movie in accorded it perhaps the highest praise it will ever receive: 'It broke my mind.' Maddin's reaction to the whole affair was oblique: 'When I think of Missoula, I think of the field that Sissy Spacek gets dragged through in the movie *Badlands,*' he revealed.
>
> Unmentioned – perhaps unknown – by the newspaper item or any of its subjects was the curious fact that Missoula, Montana, is not just any small midwestern city, but the birthplace of none other than David Lynch. How this may connect with the popularity of Maddin's film there is unclear, but what may be almost certain is that a screening of *Blue Velvet* would not have had the same effect. It isn't weird enough, and, more to the point, is almost completely lacking in mountains.

In fact, we Missoulians are very aware of the Lynch connection: for years we claimed *Blue Velvet* was inspired by another local theatre, the Wilma, or rather events that supposedly took place in its upstairs apartments. You should have heard the ruckus when Lynch himself debunked this cherished bit of local lore in an interview with our weekly paper.

Walking home after the Flatlanders concert, George's wife, Melissa, mentioned that we'd been standing ten feet away from Caelum for most of the show. I found this somewhat disheartening. From the moment we'd arrived in Winnipeg I'd been intently scrutinizing groups of people, scanning for faces from the Maddin filmography. I was disappointed not to have noticed the actor whose line in *Careful* was the memorable 'Master has an occluded bowel. Fetch Herr Doktor Schmidt.' Maddin's movies make Winnipeg seem like a very small place, like you might round any corner and run into Kyle McCulloch or Victor Cowie or Brent Neale – all important and beloved civic figures in the Winnipeg of my imagination.

In any event, *Careful* didn't save the New Crystal Theater for long. It closed about a year after Caelum's book came out. Naturally, there was much civic wailing and hand-wringing about the loss of our spunky little art house, mostly from the same hypocrites who talk a big game about local this and culture that, and then always have to stay home and wash their hair or something.

Maddin was running late for breakfast and joined us at the pancake house after the rest of us had already ordered. The first thing out of his mouth after introductions was an anecdote about bringing his elderly mother to the set of his Dracula movie the day before. She'd tripped over some cables and started to fall when Guy reached out and caught her. 'I haven't felt those breasts for forty years,' he said, looking incredulous but happy, like he'd just stepped unscathed out of a minor car accident. And he came bearing gifts: video copies of *The Heart of the World* and *Odilon Redon*, both unavailable on DVD at the time. That afternoon we picked him up at his house and went on a tour of the *Dracula: Pages from a Virgin's Diary* set. George doesn't drive, so I found myself, a not particularly good driver either, shuttling the conjoined brains behind my movie

obsession to a disused mattress warehouse with the same queasy feeling one gets high up on a chairlift, reflecting that it would take but a single impulsive heave of the buttocks to lunge into oblivion. Strangely, I never thought to ask them if they were accustomed to this kind of idolatry-based tourism. I do remembering inquiring after the lispiest intersection in Winnipeg, my favourite in Missoula being Lester and Sussex. George said he'd think on it, and Guy suggested that the most Nabokovian, anyway, would be Portsmouth and Ramsgate, revealing not only his agility of thought, but also the extent to which he and George were prepared to indulge my nerdish attempts at small talk.

Nowadays, of course, I can tell people that my association with Guy Maddin is really just a tale of successful stalking. Practically a testimonial for stalking, actually. It's been a wonderful saga to reflect on. I can call myself a Maddin collaborator, but at heart I'm still just an adoring fan. If the pattern holds, I'll see him again in 2013. The night before leaving Winnipeg, Sarah and I hooked up with Guy one last time at an outdoor café off Corydon. I don't remember a thing we talked about, but he gave us his email and told us to keep in touch. I took him at his word and came back to Montana fit to bust with Super-8 ambitions. For three or four years I sent him a copy of every new thing I finished, mostly music videos for local bands, and he was always very enthusiastic, very generous in his critiques (George, on the other hand, could be merciless).

One day in early 2006 I just happened to call him while he was planning a montage of angry strikers marching in lockstep past

St. Mary's Academy for Girls, the entire sequence to pulsate with 'pudendal throbbings' from within. A laundry list of animation possibilities quickly grew out of those first throbbings: amusement parks, bison stampedes, trench warfare and frozen horses. Guy encouraged me to keep rooting around Winnipeg's past for inspiration and egged me on to transform my findings however I liked. 'Just run something by me and I'll likely tell you to help yourself to creating that image,' was the full extent of his orders.

It was fun working like that, exchanging decayed bits of Winnipeg imagery across the border. He sent me a copy of *Winnipeg 100*, a souvenir photo album published to coincide with the city's 1973 centennial, which became my primary reference. In fact, here I must congratulate myself a little for rescuing If Day from the dustbin of history by noticing a tiny picture of it in *Winnipeg 100* and innocently asking Guy if he had anything in mind for it. He'd never heard of it! No one had. Evidently no one in Winnipeg ever mentioned the time 5,000 Rotarians in rented Nazi uniforms staged a mock occupation and renamed the city Himmlerstadt. Just never came up. A nice photographer named Cliff Eyland came along with George and Guy on some of our Winnipeg outings in 2001, but the pictures he later sent me were mostly from inside the mattress factory. I myself didn't take any pictures, and I don't recall a single bit of Winnipeg architecture first-hand. When I think about scenery on that trip, I think of the water-taxi ride with George on a sun-dappled Red River, no buildings at all, just tree-lined banks and air thick with mosquitoes and dreamy summer haze. But as I was preparing the animation for *My Winnipeg*, I decided I wanted to reach out to the If Day generation, the thinning ranks of Winnipeggers old enough to remember the event even if they didn't remember it or see the point in talking about it. *Winnipeg 100* had pages of long-gone schools and breweries, gingerbread city halls and fabulous flat-iron luxury hotels, and in my creative megalomania I got it in my head to restore these vanished skylines to *My Winnipeg*, to resurrect them in silhouette for elderly residents bussed to the theatre from senior centres and managed-care facilities. Well, it was that plus the usual tangle of selfish motives that go along with the creative urge, which as Maddin says is actually only half an urge to create and half a narcissistic urge to be adored. I wanted to impress Guy and George obviously, and hopefully ingratiate myself to any associates of theirs with real Canadian money to spend on future animations. Still, I'm dead serious when I say I also looked at *My Winnipeg* as an opportunity to give something back to Winnipeg, flatter its ego a bit, offer a few jolts of recognition, bewitch its residents with phantasmic glimpses of an idealized past. And I do expect them to love me for it. Because really, as Guy says, there are no limits to the self-centredness of a filmmaker.

Andy Smetanka first started cutting silhouettes as a means of coping with the nervousness of impending fatherhood. He lives and works on an 1890s homestead in Missoula, Montana, with his wife and their two sons.

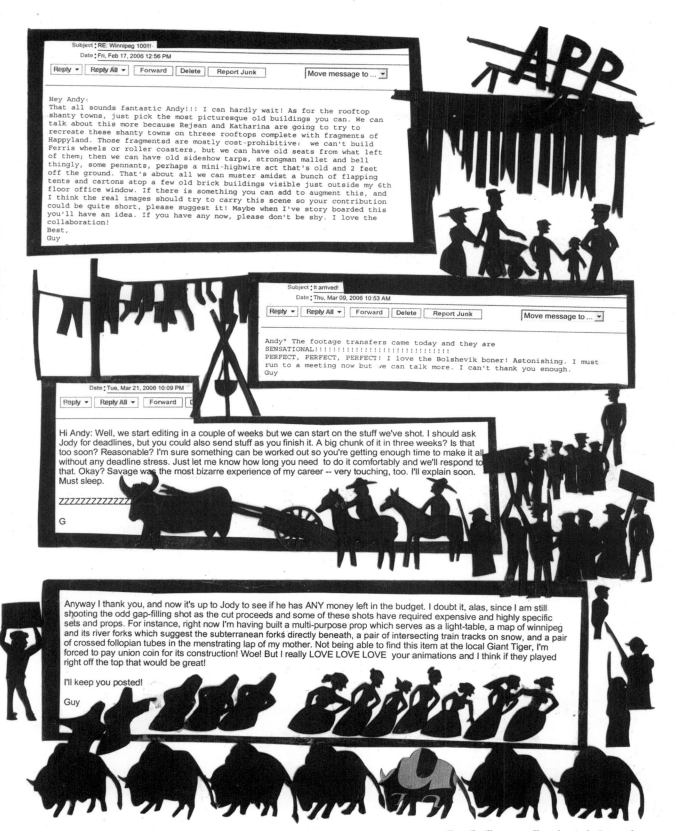

Email–silhouette collage by Andy Smetanka

Glad you're loving this! The fake Nazi occupation is, well, not quite that. There's a cool sequence in Michael Powell's 49th Parallel set in Winnipeg, with German spies looking for pie in various diners. Or are you speaking of something you found in Winnipeg 100?

Your insert contributions to Happyland will be most prized! And your skylines, too. I must congratulate myself for talking you ijnto this!

Today Katharina discovered 25 minutes of 16mm footage of the Holly Snow Shoe Club of Wpg on their 30th anniversary frolics in 1935. Three hundred sbnow shoers dancings, playing hockey, curling in blackface, dancing in dress shoes on an indoor rink, all very strange and innocent and moving! I'm going to rewatch it right now!

Cheers,

Guy

Andy: Here are some really strange bison shots taken here in Winnipeg about 90 yrs ago.

Ever since you mentioned that fake Nazi invasion last weekend, there has been an explosion of talk about it around here. Last Sunday was its 64th anniversary. It was known as If Day, and Wpg was the only city to hold one -- a complete seige of the city by 3500 soldiers. The premier, mayor and school principals were all arrested and put in a concentration camp set up at a local fort. The newspapers were seized and renamed and the main street renamed after Hitler. There were bookburnings and bullyings! Why in Winnipeg?

G

Glad you caught those sad bison.

Now, the SMAGs should probably be in the teen range: 14-17

It's probably too late, and I don't care about historical accuracy, but if it helps you to know, then I'll tell you that SMAG was once surrounded on all sides by a wrought iron spiked fence. I'm not sure what years this fence was up. It may have gone up after 1919; it was just taken down, but not before a recent late-night motorcyclist was hurled from his speeding hog, impaled upon this girls' fence, and hung there until he was discovered pinned like a bug on display outside the dorms.

G

Fancies from Wonderful Winnipeg
by Darcy Fehr

People always want to know how Guy came to choose me as his celluloid self. I wonder if Guy even knows. Sometimes I rehearse the questions I would ask him but I dare not in case the blessing is broken. Of course, I don't have a clue – I can only dream one up. Guy once pointed out that sometimes directors come about their casting decisions in roundabout ways, without audition rooms or demo reels or fanaticism, that sometimes these decisions are left to the murky and muddy waters of the Forks beneath the Forks.

But there's an element of destiny to our relationship, at least for me – one long-ago trip to Toronto that sealed our fates. On April 12, 2002, I was on a streetcar heading north on Spadina. I was hopeless, prepared to call it quits on the performance world forever, like I had decided before I left Winnipeg. I had walked about thirty kilometres that day, Day 15 of the expedition, dropping off photos and resumés to talent agencies and following up on a dozen places I had sent

SASES to before leaving Winnipeg. All letters had led to naught so far, and every heavy door swooshed shut behind me day after miserable day. My brand-new fake-leather dress shoes from Eaton's Place back home were taking a toll on my already very sore heels. The band-aids were settled at the arches of my feet, now covering the holes of my 'lucky' socks. Three weeks earlier, I had left my family – wife Krysia and daughter Kaiit – back in the 'Peg and committed myself to the Big Smoke for six weeks to find a talent agent. I planned to return to Winnipeg on my daughter's fifth birthday, May 4, with an armful of hope for Daddy's helplessly flailing acting career. If there was none, I was hanging up my raw heels and getting store credit for those shoes.

I decided to take a different path that day so I could see a little bit more of the

175

Asylum before I left. Yonge to Eglinton and a bus was the suggested 'safe' route for this small-city boy, but it was the middle of the day, after all, and I was not expected for hours. I liked the old streetcars better, anyway. They were like giant gondolas of yesterT.O. swaying effortfully through the rapidly changing concrete-scape. I found a vacant double seat when I boarded; I deliberately saved the window seat for some right person who would come along, and I was exhaling hope as each stop picked up new pairs of averted eyes. Giving up on the soul suck at Dundas, I slid over to the vacant seat and scooped up the *NOW* magazine that some somnambulist had left behind. I started flipping through it and suddenly got an inkling to see a movie: a house made of light was the perfect place to hide for a few hours. I turned to the movie listings and started scanning titles and locations. I would have to ask the driver for directions if I found something interesting.

And then my heart skipped a beat. Right there, listed under the Images Festival of Independent Film and Video, was the fateful fact that Guy Maddin was in town that evening for a curated event titled Guy Maddin Presents. I had worked with Guy before; in fact, the first film I ever did was with Maddin: *The Cock Crew or Love-Chaunt of the Chimney* back in 1997 (which has become the *Love-Chaunt Workbooks*, four shorts available on the *Cowards Bend the Knee* DVD). After I

came in to do some pickup shots, on account of my poor performance, he asked me to do a short, *Hospital Fragment*, a special feature for the *Tales from the Gimli Hospital* DVD released by Kino Video in 2000.

Maddin believed in me – he always gave me so much freedom to try things and would never call me down from that chimney, even when my head was swirling with insecurities and fears and Merlot. Yes, I would see Guy and he would talk to me here in this godforsaken loony bin and maybe, maybe, *maybe* I could get him to write me a reference letter to get an agent! My body filled with new-found life! My pants swelled with charged eroticism!! I sprang to my feet and fondled my way to the front, getting furtive glances from some and surprisingly succumbing swoons from others. I confidently asked the driver, 'Can you tell me how to get to Sussex Avenue?'

His reply: 'That's the next stop, sir.'

When someone asks me how Guy came to his decision about me, I mostly reply, 'I'm not sure.'

Darcy Fehr is an actor, instructor and filmmaker happily nestled away in wonderful Winnipeg with his family of four: Christina Angela, Kaiit Alyssa, Aedyn Justus and resident canine, Marcus Barkus.

— CBC RADIO PLAY w/ live audience

- Olivia de Havilland, Anne Savage, Lizabeth Scott.
- zeppelins!

- The need to swim the river !!!

Snow
Blossoms (F) The beauty of snow drifts ^{w/flowers} ; Frondes Agrestis p.128
                      & MONTAGE
- Radio play: Fauré, Mk, Ball.

(LA) — Rituals help memory: coming out to log
sunrises + sunsets each day.

☆ MOST IMP: DARCY plays me @
<u>all</u> ages, even as a child, so that
childhood colleagues & crushes may
be 12, while I am 30. (Ferdydurke
(5)☆ & the Sherbrook hard-on-boys & the
bullies slapping me around are all 12)

(S) — Sherbrook pool = Nude swimming in
3rd Basement pool.
(S) — Life giving @ second
(S) — Regular swimming on main.

(Mother to TV Son) 1.

(In spite of what you think,
you have never been a disappoint to me!

2. When you were a (child model) for Hudson's Bay
I was so full of PRIDE I could hardly
Breathe. (That little check suite) and
not a hair out of place!

3.   Mother continues
If you want to quit your Job and
lie around like a "Pasha" from now on
I'll buy extra pillows for the Sofa,
I'll pick up your soiled clothes and
do the laundry, if you are too busy.
You won't have to lift a finger

4. I will never again accuse you of stealing
change from my purse.

                              Not me
5. It is for you to decide if the lawn need
mowing. Even if it looks like
a jungle out there and the neighbors —
complain, I won't ask, I will hire a boy
to do it or do it my self

turn to next Page ————————→

Ann Savage's dialogue in her own handwriting

178

Strange Direction
by Caelum Vatnsdal

At some point near the end of the 1980s, articles on the theme of eccentricity began to appear in the Canadian entertainment press. More specifically, these articles tried first to document and then to explain the proliferation of 'prairie Surrealist' films being produced by a dozen-year-old film co-operative called the Winnipeg Film Group. A small group of directors working within that organization, the writers claimed, were responsible. As the decade came to a close, analysts concluded that one of them in particular, an ex-banker with a commerce degree named Guy Maddin, was the alpha dog on whom the ultimate responsibility for prairie Surrealism should be pinned.

Since his first feature, 1988's *Tales from the Gimli Hospital,* Maddin has contributed more than thirty weird motion pictures, in both short and feature form, to the world's ever-growing supply. His directorial techniques are unlike those of any other filmmaker, past, present and, one might reasonably predict, future. These singular means, impossible to ascribe to any one school, result in singular films: super-artificial fantasias on superannuated genres, products of an incredibly specific geographic location and social circle. There are no other movies like them being made.

In viewing a Maddin picture, it's hard not to assume there must have been some strange alchemy on the set – they seem woven and filigreed or blown like smoke rings rather than simply, bluntly 'shot' as other movies are; one would be forgiven for assuming they were magicked together by a team of pillow-sleeved artistes sipping absinthe and puffing on clove-and-hashish cigarettes, presided over by a rouged and beret-clad Maddin shrieking directions in falsetto from a diamond-velvet throne floating atop a dais of honeyed mist.

This depiction is fanciful, but only just. It's true Maddin's concoctions are not made the same way as other movies, which typically feature barking ADs, crews of almost martial discipline and frantic underlings scurrying about like silverfish. One can't imagine these industry hierarchies and noisy caste systems resulting in such strange execrations as

Archangel or *Careful,* and indeed they don't. But neither were Maddin's pictures sneezed into existence by an elf: any movie, however chimerical, requires a team of people working in concert to solve an array of practical, reality-based problems; so it follows that there must be some method on a Maddin set, magical or otherwise, to replace the joyless Hollywood system.

Following are four glimpses into the curious world of Guy Maddin and his exceedingly strange direction.

The Cock Crew
Summer 1997

The set of Maddin's short film *The Cock Crew* served as, if nothing else, a compressed representation of all his sets before and since. It was, for those who were there, a greatest-hits collection of the renowned filmmaker's weird and eccentric filmmaking methods: a hundred-proof distillation of his singular talents, made all the more intoxicating, in retrospect, for having never resulted in an actual finished film.

The Cock Crew was conceived as a sort of response to chapter 94 of *Moby-Dick*, 'A Squeeze of the Hand,' in which the jolly whalers of the Pequod sit around a vat of whale sperm and squash the lumps out of it. 'A sweet and unctuous duty!' enthuses Melville's Ishmael. Maddin and his scenarist George Toles had found inspiration in another Melville composition too, a short story of melancholy and fowl obsession called 'Cock-a-Doodle-Doo.' Thus the presence on-set of a rooster nicknamed Rochester who, according to the script, is meant, with his ceaseless crowing, to erotically charge the owner, lady and sallow female employees of a tiny mom-and-pop paper mill.

The main set built in the small studio is a chimney, bulging and bricky, and a cottage/factory interior furnished with great pulp vats, stick furniture and a perch for the rooster. In a bold gambit the crew never really understood, the walls were painted like cuts of meat. Perhaps this was to evoke the marbled cross-sections of whale meat described in Melville's opus, or else was meant to give a greasy, organic, T-boned sheen to the proceedings. Despite multiple discussions on the subject and several oblique interrogations of the director, the crew never settled on whether this idea had come from Maddin or someone else entirely – someone random who had proposed it as a joke, with Maddin, believing it a serious suggestion, too embarrassed or gullible to reject it out of hand. That they never discovered the provenance of the notion was by specially crafted design. It lent a vague multiplicity to the movie's authorship, which in turn gave Maddin an excuse to not have all the answers. This was only one of the psychological ploys applied by the director in the making of *The Cock Crew*.

Devious mind games are one of Maddin's most important and oft-used, yet least documented, techniques. To be sure, he is far from the first director to employ psychological manipulation in the making of his films – stories abound of this or that Hollywood martinet setting actors against one another for onscreen effect, or surreptitiously rolling basketballs into the shot in order to persuade a recalcitrant starlet that one more take was needed – but it was Maddin who pioneered the notion of taking this approach to every crew member, from the top-billed star down to the lowliest daily set painter. On *The Cock Crew* he started early, on the very first day of pre-production, by implanting suggestions of a mysterious cabal of 'executive producers' who were somewhere deep behind the scenes, holding the purse strings and making the important decisions. They were touchy, Maddin claimed, and fiercely parsimonious; also notoriously impossible to predict but omnipotent: anything that might happen over the three weeks to come would therefore not be Maddin's fault. Bad things would happen only in spite of him.

More important than the psychological gambits Maddin used were the sensory embellishments he pioneered. To build the mood of his picture, Maddin played music almost constantly through pre-production, always keeping a weather eye on the Victrola lest some amateur DJ throw down an incongruous platter. Most of the tunes Maddin kept in rotation were those you'd expect: anything from 'Dodging a Divorcée' by Ambrose and his Orchestra to 'Love, You Funny Thing' by Der Bingle, to something by Mance Lipscomb, Russ Columbo or Fred Waring's Pennsylvanians. Occasionally the older music was interrupted by a loud blast of Cheap Trick, a rare Blue Öyster Cult bootleg or else sounds Maddin had recorded by sleeve microphone in the geriatric wards of the local hospital. Brick by brick, a unique aural backdrop was erected about the proceedings, to the occasional consternation of the WFG staff.

All the senses were catered to on *The Cock Crew*. Before the first workers even trouped into the empty studio, Maddin painstakingly scented the air with his arsenal of colour-coded spray bottles. A soft purple bottle held the delicate smell of lilac while a pink one flecked with black produced *odeur du pastèque*. Other, more obscure smells hung in drifts here or there throughout the studio; some of them, Maddin claimed, had been produced in *dix-septième* France and preserved over the centuries in airtight glass bells, which Maddin had purchased some years earlier at the estate sale of a renowned Hollywood queen.

The process of scenting was repeated each morning and again at lunchtime, and so the whole day long, great cloud banks of violet, spice and watermelon elbowed each other for airspace. Other odours the director employed were less pleasant, and were held in reserve for serious punishment scenarios. Whenever the artists toiling to make props and set pieces lagged in their labours or produced shoddy work, Maddin's lips would tighten in anger and he would dig into his stained canvas duffel bag for an ugly spray can with a peeled label and rusted bottom. He would hit the trigger and spin in circles, and the horrible stink of rotten eggs would fill the air, obliterating the delicate perfumes and sending the builders, technicians and actors – everybody, in fact, but

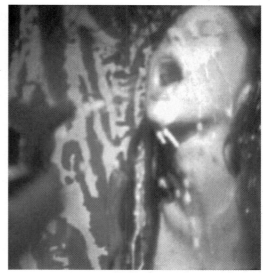

Maddin – reeling away, hacking and retching. His grim duty done, Maddin would stalk out, down three flights to the street and across to a lunch counter called Soup and Sandwich Heaven, where he would order coffee and brood for precisely three quarters of an hour. On his return he always found the crew working at double time amid the lingering ribbons of stench, eager to do whatever it took to stave off their boss's anger in future.

But Maddin is a peace-loving man, and these incidents were rare. His sensory craftsmanship was, in the main, exquisite. He hired a servant named Kym, a young and delicate flower of unexampled androgyny, to cater to the crew's needs. At each noontime, Kym's job was to first uncork several bottles of white wine and then halve a dozen sweet grapefruits. These were served at a long table covered in a white cloth, upon which Kym had already laid out Maddin's mother's silver and china. Serrated spoons, that cherished tool of the grapefruit devotee, were ready at every place. Maddin saw that the music was turned up and the scents were fresh, and that upon every seat there was a velvet pillow. And over the days the sets grew, sprouting into a magical, meaty fairyland that would be destined never to see the light of a projector bulb.

Maddin maintained this crazily crafted world for five solid weeks. It became a lifestyle for the crew, and something of an addiction. They spent most hours of the day in a world they had literally built, and there seemed no good reason to leave it. They had all the wine they could drink and all the grapefruit they could eat, and Kym's androgynous charms appealed to everyone. It seemed at the time an end in itself: half installation piece, half Actionist 'happening,' half party, with Maddin the courtliest of hosts. (Yes, that is three halves, but in some cases, certainly in this one, the wonderful, horrible trauma and joy of unbound creativity can trump common mathematics.) So it was, in the end, no surprise to anyone when a coherent movie failed to materialize from the white-wine-and-perfume-soaked haze.

Twilight of the Ice Nymphs
Summer 1996

A year before *The Cock Crew* came a film that was not made under quite the same serene and modest circumstances, and in fact was a sufficiently opposite experience for Maddin that the carefully crafted utopia of the later short may be seen as a direct response. A relatively lavish production, the feature film *Twilight of the Ice Nymphs* was a monstrous trial for the filmmaker: everything that could go wrong, it seemed, went wrong twice.

The budget for this film was more than anything Maddin had been given before, and he resolved to make use of it, planning for an incredibly lush and busy forest environment – the ever-twilit kingdom of Mandragora – that was to be shot on his customary distressed 16mm film. Powers above him (this time there really was a faraway cabal of capricious and almighty producers) dictated the film should be shot on 35mm film, which at once widened and clarified the frame Maddin had to fill and, because the 35mm stock and equipment were incredibly expensive, deprived him of the means to fill it.

In the weeks leading up to the shoot, Maddin began experiencing a series of strange nightmares. Already suffering from a neurological condition that caused him to feel he was constantly being prodded by invisible fingers, Maddin found them nearly impossible to deal with. He was, in each dream, atop some desert stone formation, towering and streaked in rust – something out of a Road Runner cartoon or a John Ford movie. His actors – faceless, as the final cast has not been settled upon – were atop one another, grouped on a mesa on the far side of the arroyo. He could barely see them, but he began yelling instructions, vainly trying to communicate his wishes over the desert wind. They were too far away; they were talking amongst themselves. This man must not know anything about directing, they laughed to one another – otherwise why would he have chosen such a far-off butte to do his directing from?

Maddin awoke from these dreams sweaty and shaking, his self-confidence utterly shattered. He could barely bring himself to wheel his penny-farthing to the studio in the morning. When he did, he was always dismayed, angry despite himself, by the progress made on the creation of Mandragora. Everyone was working hard on this one – it was, after all, a professional movie shoot, and the crew were being paid real wages – but there was only so much that could be done with the resources left to the art department after the 35mm camera had hoovered up the lion's share of the money.

Halfway through pre-production, Maddin's neurological disorders began manifesting themselves physically. Mandragora transformed slowly into a tempest-toss'd Mediterranean island, with Maddin its Prospero conjuring up storms and creatures the likes of which the world had never seen. The studio, a cavernous old warehouse previously used to store garbage, became infested with all manner of entities, from ghosts (as when a terrified Maddin spied the shimmering shade of Red Alix, a long-dead Winnipeg radio sportscaster) to gargantuan flies and fire ants. Crew members were attacked without warning. First assistant director Richard O'Brian-Moran felt a crawling sensation on his chest and clawed off his shirt to reveal a moving bib of ants covering his rib cage, which he mashed into a blackberry-jam paste. Soon after that, art director Ian Handford was beset by the parasites and spent the better part of the day squatting helplessly behind a tree in the spurious loam of the studio pulling a stock ticker's worth of tapeworms from his fundament.

Maddin stumbled around in the midst of all this, expressing horror and sympathy at the various mishaps, but no real surprise. 'Mrs. Bustaffo,' an invisible alter ego he had conjured up some years earlier as a scapegoat for his more outré decisions, screamed helpful 'suggestions' in his head. There was a funhouse aspect to the studio: insect and ghost attacks on the crew redoubled, and disembodied wails emanated from the cavernous dark so often they soon become just another part of the low-budget scenery. The producer, who suffered a number of minor injuries himself (a falling

fake tree to the skull one day, a sound clobbering by a firehose gone wild the next), wandered about like Caliban, occasionally looming wide-eyed from the gloam to startle crew members with his aphasic gibbering and increasing dishevelment. Superficially, the studio had become a cheap carnival house of horrors, but, for those contractually bound to be there every day, and particularly for Maddin, there was, beneath all that, a profound miasma of despair no sideshow attraction could match.

The producer's inarticulateness was contagious, and soon Maddin found himself having trouble issuing his directions. Simple commands such as 'Action!' and 'Cut!' came out, in one delirious case, as 'Ah-groo!' and 'Bonk-bonk-bonk!' To cover this, or at least to make it seem more deliberate, Maddin affected further eccentricities, many of them suggested to him by the unseen Mrs. Bustaffo. Sartorial flourishes such as a lab coat, thick round goggles and a large tobacco pipe upholstered in rabbit fur gave him the appearance of a thoroughgoing crackpot, while, he found, rendering him more comfortable on-set. When queried about the costume, he would smile slyly, shuffle his feet and defensively mutter something about Fritz Lang. '*Lang* wore goggles,' Maddin might croak, 'and a lab coat too!'

The film was eventually finished despite a tell-all book's worth of tragedies, turnabouts and disasters. But even given the energy and enthusiasm and sick, sick love put into the project by everyone involved, and a creditable release by the distributor, the final product was, to its creator, in every respect a failure. At the premiere, held at the famous Towne Cinema 8 in Winnipeg,

Jeff Solylo photographing Kyle McCulloch in Careful

Maddin found himself caught deep in the centre section of the seating, far away from any potential escape route. As he sat there, trapped, watching the film he knew and loathed so well, all his neuroses and afflictions returned at full strength. Hundreds of fingers poked at him; strange odours invaded his nostrils; voices in his brain screamed that he was talentless, terrible, incompetent – a hack! The image onscreen was slightly out of focus and the sound was much too low, but in Maddin's tortured mind there was no focus at all, just a wash of pastel and indecipherably faint mumbling sounds, and he began to feel physically ill. He was sitting beside one of the lead actors, Shelley Duvall, and so fought to maintain his composure to avoid alarming the cheerful but fragile-seeming star, whose simple but delicious recipes, liberally dispensed during the shoot, had accounted for a high percentage of whatever joy Maddin derived from the ordeal.

The movie was ninety-two minutes long, but to Maddin the fuzzy mess seemed to grind on forever. On its national release, the movie was saddled with a bad poster (a picture of an ostrich wearing a feather boa and the nonsensical tagline 'One Man's Search for Amorous Requital in a Land Where the Sun Never Sets') and poor reviews, where it was reviewed at all. Maddin's most lavish and expensive production was also his least personal, and more than a decade later it remains his most complete failure. Considering it's

competing for that title with several movies that were never even finished or released, that's saying an awful lot.

Careful
Summer 1991

Maddin's third feature film, shot in yet another Winnipeg warehouse over the summer of 1991, provides us with yet more evidence of the singularity of this director's process. In these early days Maddin's techniques were more primitive, and more grounded. This was before the neuropathies, before Mrs. Bustaffo, before the bottled scents. The set of *Careful* was run more like a day camp or a vacation at the lake than one of B. F. Skinner's operant conditioning chambers, as in later films.

The cast and crew were encouraged to find pictures they liked and stick them on the wall of the studio's green room (actually a walled-in enclosure decorated with shag-carpet scraps and Christmas lights). Maddin also called for theme days that, he hoped, would unite the crew together in hatred of them. At first, however, they were a big hit. There was Bring Your Own Chair Day, on which the excited artisans roared into the rutted dirt parking lot with a variety of ugly chairs strapped to the tops of their Galaxies, Chevelles and Rancho Deluxes. Someone suggested a Funny Hat Day, but Maddin shot the idea down as timid and banal, countering with Relapse Day, a day on which everyone in the crew was to indulge in any substance to which they might at one time have been addicted, nearly addicted or dangerously attracted. Not much work was done on Relapse Day, but the slurring, giggling crew raised a hearty toast to 'the best movie director in the world!' before staggering off into the far corners of the studio to vomit behind the half-built *papier-mâché* mountains.

The Day of Reckoning, another brainchild of Maddin's, was held only a day or two before the start of principal photography. On this special day, any grievances formed in pre-production were aired, and offenders subjected to some appropriate punishment concocted by a panel of supposedly impartial and grievance-free crew members. Most of the crimes were minor, but there were several for which the panel meted out rough justice. One crew member was imprisoned inside a tiny train car that was then nailed shut, leaving him only a tiny portico at the top to stare forlornly through. The little caboose had been decorated with sticks and bramble on the outside, which had been nailed into the plywood walls of the vehicle. The points of the nails poked through to the interior, and the crew member – a bewildered sets labourer on his first film job – could barely move without scratching himself bloody. The car was hooked up to a large bull ox that was part of the farm menagerie, and the beast was marched around the studio as the worker tried desperately not to be thrown against the pointy walls within. Suddenly the ox was spooked by something – a mouse perhaps, or the wild jeering of the hungover crew – and he reared up and bolted forward. The train car flipped on its side and was dragged for several feet. The harness broke – a blessing for the man in the box – and the ox tore off into a flimsy set meant to represent the entrance to a mine. The upended train car teetered for a moment and threatened to tumble down once more, but instead it spun gently and came to rest. The animal handlers rushed off to collect their stampeding ox while the train car was pried open and the worker, dazed, torn and bleeding, was led gently to a sofa in the green room. Bactine was applied liberally, and Maddin soon declared the grateful victim absolved of all sin.

Maddin's mischievous side came even further to the fore the next day. Some of his pranks seemed barely legal, and others downright dangerous, but all of them were funny. The warehouse in this case was a disused grain elevator, and in the middle of it was a one-man lift that used a pulley and counterweights to raise workers up to the loftiest heights of the ceiling. It was weighted with husky labourers in mind, so unless the rider exerted total control over the ropes, the rickety device shot up at a frightening speed. With the first days of shooting, the studio was invaded by a small army of film technicians, and a gleeful Maddin sensed prey – a whole group of people yet unacquainted with the lethality of the little elevator. One by one, he led fresh victims to the tiny lift, pretending bewilderment at some technical problem or other, the solving of which required an ascent in the contraption. Invariably, the trusting foil would ask how the elevator worked, and Maddin gave them sketchy if not outright misleading instructions. Each victim in turn rocketed skyward with a pitiable wail, many of them suffering rope burns in their desperate efforts to slow the thing down. As the elevator crashed into its upper resting place with an echoing clang and a billow of grain dust and dry pigeon droppings, Maddin cackled with glee and called up his specially prepared bon mot: 'I guess that's why they call it a *dumb*waiter!'

There were other japes, most of them masterminded by the director. Before a nude bathing scene involving two actors, he poured several bottles of blue dye into the pool set. When the actors emerged, shivering and stained azure, Maddin explained that he had merely wanted the water to look 'as wet as possible,' but no one missed the impish gleam in his eye. Two days later, a stranger appeared on-set: an old man wearing sunglasses, a porkpie hat and an overcoat, and sporting a long white beard. No one could work up the courage to approach

On the set of My Winnipeg *with First Assistant Director Ronaldo Nacionales*

the mumbling senior, and Maddin, the one all agreed should perform the eviction, could not be found. Finally, the film's producers, Greg Klymkiw and Tracy Traeger, confronted the old man together. The stranger opened his coat, flung away his hat and pulled down the false beard: it was Maddin himself, with painted-on wrinkles, cackling wildly! He capered and cavorted in the unbridled sea-dog style that would become a familiar sight.

After a week or so of shooting, the out-of-town actors arrived (including Australian director Paul Cox and Canadian television mainstay Jackie Burroughs), and Maddin found he had less time for tricks and fancies. But he had noted the effect of his pranks on the cast and crew – they seemed to have brought everyone to his wavelength, to have made them realize this was not to be just another low-budget film production. A quick-witted and observant man, as most filmmakers are, he began to realize how easy it could be to manipulate a group of people by fomenting an atmosphere of hyper-reality, magic and celestial whim.

Careful was a watershed film in Maddin's development as an *artiste planant*, a term of his own private coinage meaning, roughly, *gliding* or *trippy* artist. After a few stumbles (a feature called *The Dikemaster's Daughter* planned but never made; a TV half-hour called *The Hands of Ida* that unfortunately was made; and, of course, the aforementioned *Twilight of the Ice Nymphs*) and several subsequent years of relative inaction,

Maddin sculpted and sanded this term into something with real meaning through the making of his short film *The Heart of the World* in 2000. The *artiste planant* style was by then fully formed, and was frequently expressed by the dancing of jigs.

My Winnipeg
Winter/Spring 2007

At the beginning of Maddin's moviemaking career, his philosophies were naturally immature, and his eccentric behaviours came instinctively and were less flagrant. During the making of his first feature, *Tales from the Gimli Hospital*, Maddin's rewards to his actors were not the heavenly scents, white wine and grapefruits of later years, but two hours of television watching and beer served in stubby bottles. As he made more films, however, and began working with people who were not in his immediate circle of friends, he learned that the more extreme the stimulus, the more extreme the results; and Maddin was certainly after extreme results. If his crews were not converted completely to his methods in this manner, then at least they were discombobulated, and therefore tractable.

From one film to the next, he sharpened his talents. Between the clumsy bribes of *Tales from the Gimli Hospital* and the sophisticated manipulations of *The Cock Crew*, Maddin grew and reinvented himself to an amazing degree. His contortions precisely mirrored his almost physical reactions to the old silent and semi-silent films he adored: a kick to the shin from some lost, beautiful German iteration of the *Alraune* tale would send Maddin into a full-body ripple that exploded on the other end in the form of colour-coded atomizers and a sudden, seismic personality shift giving him the will to use them.

That was amazing enough. But *The Cock Crew* was a culmination, or so it has seemed in the decade since its making. Maddin made many films in that time and all of them had some aspect of dementia, but the on-set madness of old had gone into retreat, and Mrs. Bustaffo was apparently all but gone. The most widely held theory among his friends and associates was that Maddin had merely refined his techniques still further, to some degree beyond the perception of others, and was practicing some kind of undetectable voodoo manipulations.

All this was the case until 2007, when Maddin began work on a Documentary Channel–commissioned piece about his hometown, a challenge the director had accepted, his anti-realist urges notwithstanding, for the opportunity to slyly make a movie about himself instead. Before it was shortened to *My Winnipeg*, the film's title had been the much more apropos *Love Me, Love My Winnipeg*, which for many years had been the city's own vaguely defensive but apt slogan.

Knowing that most reputable documentaries are the product of exhaustive research and investigation, the ever-perverse Maddin chose instead to try to forget everything about his film's subject, inasmuch as it was possible to do so. He embarked on a program of alcoholism (Maddin is not typically a heavy drinker) and hallucinogens, and read as much as he could about places other than Winnipeg. After four months of this, he sobered up and made a list of the few facts about Winnipeg he could still call to mind; these became the basis for the screenplay of *My Winnipeg*. It helped that Maddin's co-writer, George Toles, had not grown up in the city and so was unable to remind the director of the schoolroom history tidbits he might have been expected to include in the piece.

Maddin had only ever considered one actress for the role of his mother, Mrs. Herdis Maddin: Ann Savage, whose insane, nail-spitting, jaw-droppingly Sadean femme-fatale performance in Edgar Ulmer's Poverty Row noir from 1945, *Detour*, had given him what he calls 'terrorections' since his first experience of it in the mid-seventies. While memories of other milestones – the loss of his virginity, for example – have been lost to the vagaries of time and strategic substance abuse, Maddin still recalls the day, hour and minute he first saw those arched eyebrows and that frowsy, maternal perm, heard that scratchy gravestone voice, felt manipulated by those whipsaw mood shifts and that bottle-blond scolding. 'I felt,' he said, 'like I was getting a spanking right through the movie screen.'

Savage, thankfully, was still alive, though she hadn't acted in over twenty years, and before that film, the 1986 drama *Fire with Fire*, had been absent from the screen for a further thirty. While some directors might have hesitated to hire an octogenarian whose acting chops might be reasonably assumed somewhat rusty, Maddin did not, because he was already prepared. Though the part was eventually played by ex-Riddler Frank Gorshin, a key role in *Twilight of the Ice Nymphs* had originally been intended for Baby LeRoy, a child actor of the thirties who, after several meaty roles as the swaddling foil to W. C. Fields, had retired at the age of six. At a certain point it had appeared that LeRoy was a lock, and the cautious Maddin had developed a card-based system inspired by the Zener cards used to test psychic abilities. His reasoning was that, faced with a superannuated actor with limited powers of memorization, it would be best to develop a small range of emotions to be delivered on-camera that could be tied to symbols. So if he wanted sadness, he could flash a picture of a star; a square would call for joy; three wiggly lines would indicate bewilderment and anger.

But LeRoy couldn't be found, and Maddin didn't get a chance to test out his cards until

Savage landed in Winnipeg a decade later. She caught on to the system immediately – Ulmer had used a similar device, it turned out – and the maiden trial of what was later dubbed the Zener-Maddin System was a roaring success.

Newly developed technology, the exigencies of a low budget and a natural human tendency toward greater efficiency obviated the need to build elaborate sets for the film, and therefore the need for yet another big warehouse studio; much of *My Winnipeg* was shot before a green screen in a tiny loft, with paintings, miniatures or archival stock footage composited in behind the actors later on. In this manner, the shooting days were often done by noon, and Maddin, along with producer Jody Shapiro (who had been drafted as the film's cinematographer when the original cameraman had quit the production in favour of a Christian TV puppet show), would retire for long, lazy afternoon naps.

Halfway through the *My Winnipeg* shoot, the naps took their toll: not on the movie itself, or on the quality of Maddin's work, but on the anarchic spirit that had once guided his directorial instincts. It was only a question of method; it could be argued that the final product was only getting better, and certainly Maddin had not become a boilerplate, ball-cap-wearing director churning product out like sausage; but to those who'd witnessed the unpredictable Maddin of old, there was something missing. It was disconcerting, and not a little melancholy, to be on a Maddin set and yet not be worried about being sprayed in the face with rotten-egg stench, locked in an iron maiden or sent up an out-of-control elevator. Maddin himself was passive and avuncular, flashing his Zener-Maddin cards with a polite smile on his face. (He took to using the cards as a way of communicating to everybody on the set, not just the actors.) It seemed the dangerously unpredictable character who had, by the strangest methods imaginable, carved out a singular film career and a legendarily odd reputation, had utterly vanished.

But he is not gone, not completely. He reappears occasionally, his cap tilted at a jaunty angle, a mischievous twinkle in his eye. On one of Maddin's most recent film shoots, for example, there was, for some, a strange time-machine effect: the opening of a window, or an aperture, to a time thirteen years earlier on the set of *The Cock Crew*. This new film, a documentary examination of Maddin's efforts to use the art of collage as an alternate method of story development known as the Keyhole Project, featured an on-set masseuse, outrageous characters in bizarre costume, erotic mischief, bison-meat hamburgers, a naked woman parading about through a hashish-scented haze and a half-ton of shredded paper scattered randomly about, all set to the musical accompaniment of hockey superstar Guy Lafleur's lost, legendary disco album *Lafleur*. The floodlight was lit and the camera whirred hungrily. Mrs. Bustaffo was in the vicinity – you could hear her breathing. The streamer guns were cocked and loaded. The old madman had awoken … the *artiste planant* lives!

Caelum Vatnsdal is a filmmaker and writer based in his own Winnipeg.

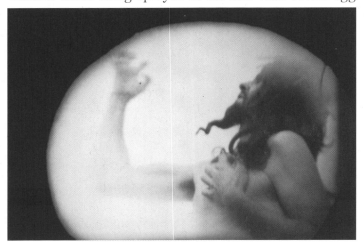

Caelum Vatnsdal as Osip in Heart of the World

Mimo   Day off to get car washed; First dinner.   RS Rear Screen

plot p.42   STORY   Tossing & turning in Bed

EMOTIONAL IMPOTENCE

I Infrastructure   Roof Top culture
Dreams of buildings, bridges, back lanes, garbage hill,
panama canal, fossils in the limestone
     Railroads linking   & Frozen Horse Heads

Early **S** Sherbrooke Pool ⑤

LA Linking Amnesia — wandering forgetfulness;
stuff that might link separate episodes

Early **D** Drone activity outside of actual events that
happen to involve Drones.   Quechua — step
          ↑   backwards
     Simon Winnipeg into Juno Beach
                       covered in darkness

½ **P** Paddlewheel episode ⑦

Early **Ch** Childbirth episode] father pees on mum's feet
                               ④

Early **B.C.** Blind Curator episode ①

early **B** Black Hearts in Arena razed ②   ③ Two houses
                                              for same
                                              Family.
                                              SMAG drinking

800 **TV** Man on a Ledge

          Montage of weather
          days & nights
          p.40

F Fog ⅋ᴮᵃᶜᵏˡⁱᵗ Breath Montage p 26

(Greenway)   Me & Miss Mandible ⑥   (P.54 Betsy)

Guy Maddin's Filmography

Night Mayor (9 min, 2009)

'Lectric Chair (7 min-loop, co-directed with Isabella Rossellini, 2009)

Glorious (12 min, 2008)

Footsteps (9 min, 2008)

Collage Party (12 min, 2008)

It's My Mother's Birthday Today (4 min, 2008)

Berlin (1 min, 2008)

Spanky – To the Pier and Back (4 min, 2008)

My Winnipeg (feature, 2007)

Odin's Shield Maiden (4 min, 2006)

Nude Caboose (2 min, 2006)

Brand upon the Brain! (feature, 2006)

My Dad Is 100 Years Old (17 min, 2005)

FuseBoy (4 min, 2005)

Sombra Dolorosa (6 min, 2005)

Sissy-Boy Slap-Party (6 min, 2004)

A Trip to the Orphanage (4 min, 2004)

The Saddest Music in the World (feature, 2003)

Cowards Bend the Knee (feature, 2003)

Fancy, Fancy Being Rich (6 min, 2002)

Dracula – Pages from a Virgin's Diary (feature, 2002)

It's a Wonderful Life (3 min, 2001)

The Heart of the World (5 min, 2000)

Hospital Fragment (3 min, 1999)

Rooster Workbook (4 min, 1997)

Zookeeper Workbook (4 min, 1997)

Chimney Workbook (4 min, 1997)

Twilight of the Ice Nymphs (feature, 1997)

Odilon Redon (5 min, 1995)

Careful (feature, 1992)

Archangel (feature, 1990)

Tales from the Gimli Hospital (feature, 1988)

The Dead Father (21 min, 1985)

Credits

Photos on pages 1, 2 (top), 4, 7, 8, 10, 11, 12, 13, 14, 15, 16–17, 19, 22, 25, 33, 36, 40, 41, 42, 45, 47, 51, 56, 60, 61, 64, 65, 67, 69, 71, 73, 74, 75, 78, 79, 80, 81, 82, 83, 85, 86, 87, 89, 90, 91, 92, 95, 99, 100, 102, 103, 105, 106, 107, 108, 112, 113, 114, 115, 116, 118, 119, 121, 122, 131, 148, 149, 153, 186 and 192 are frame grabs from *My Winnipeg*. Jody Shapiro was the director of photography.

Photos on pages 2 (bottom), 14, 18, 20, 21, 22, 23, 25, 27, 28, 29, 32, 34, 36, 38, 42, 57, 59, 72, 76, 77, 84, 91, 92, 95, 98, 124, 126, 127, 129, 134, 135, 141, 147 and 156 are from the Maddin family album.

Photos on pages 5, 31, 98, 122, 160 and 178 are from the Ann Savage Trust. Thanks to Kent Adamson.

Pages 6, 17, 177, 188 and 189 are from Guy Maddin's *My Winnipeg* notebook.

Photos on pages 8, 32, 45, 56, 87, 92, 111, 117 and 123 are by unidentified photographers.

The artists of the preparatory collages, pages 12, 46, 48, 49, 52, 53, 54, 55, 60, 62–63, 90, 94, 105, 106, 114, 116, 120, 157 and 162 are identified in captions.

Student card, p. 14, by Ross Parke, a Winnipeg Maroon.

Silhouettes, pages 18, 44, 50, 80, 115, 159 and 163, and collages, pages 173 and 174, by Andy Smetanka.

Floor plan, p. 24, by Herdis Maddin.

'SAD' photo, p. 25, by Walter Forsberg.

Photos on pages 31, 50, 53, 66, 70, 78, 97, 109, 113, 114, 118, 138, 142, 144, 146, 151, 177, 179 and 180 are by Guy Maddin.

Photos, pages 37, 50, 58, 106, 135, by Jody Shapiro.

Photo, p. 39, by Lennie Bijokis.

Photo of Noam Gonick, p. 44, by Larry Glawson.

Photos, pages 64 and 69, by Bruce Monk.

X-ray, p. 70, by unidentified lab technician.

Painting, p. 88, by Cris Cleen.

Photos, pages 93, 132, 133, 168, 171, by Jeff Solylo.

Photo, p. 101, by Barney Charach.

Photo, p. 136, by Rebecca Sandulak.

Photos, pages 139 and 143, by Adam L. Weintraub.

Illustration, p. 150, by Krimo.

Artwork, pages 154–5, by Marcel Dzama, *Untitled (Winnipeg Map)*, 2007, Graphite, pen, and ink on sketchbook page, 2-part drawing (each: 27.9 x 21.3

cm; 35.2 x 50.8 x 2.5 cm), courtesy of the artist and David Zwirner, New York.

Posters, pages 164–5, by Keller House. Top left buffalo by Guy Maddin. Top right p. 164 by Soda Pictures UK. Blue horse poster under Guy's buffalo one is by Jody Shapiro.

Photos, pages 167, 172 and 183, by Michael Marshall.

Photo, p. 175, by Richardo Alms.

Photo, p. 184, by Kari Moffatt.

Photo, p. 187, by Deco Dawson.

Acknowledgements

Some of these annotations and collages appeared in a different form in *Border Crossings* magazine, Issue #107, August 2008, in the article 'My (Other) Winnipeg: Excerpts from a Phantom Film.'

Some of the section on Mulchy's Syndrome appeared in a different form in the Winnipeg Art Gallery catalogue for the exhibit *Subconscious City*, curated by Shawna Dempsey and Lorri Millan, February 8 to May 11, 2008.

A considerably shorter version of 'Savage Genius' appeared in the *London Guardian.*

I'd like to thank editor and designer Alana Wilcox.

Also:
E1 Entertainment: Charlotte Mickie, Bryan Gliserman
The Documentary Channel
IFC Films: Ryan Werner, Jonathan Sehring
Soda Pictures
Michael Burns
Manitoba Film and Music
Plug In ICA
Phyllis Laing
John Gurdebeke
Andy Smetanka

Jody Shapiro

Herdis Maddin
Ross Maddin
Janet Maddin
Jilian Maddin
Ann Savage
Kent Adamson

Noam Gonick
Jonah Corne

Bob Nixon
Paul Butler
Caelum Vatnsdal
Meeka Walsh
Shawna Dempsey
Lorri Millan
Marcel Dzama
Michael Ondaatje
Robert Enright
Dennis Bartok
Eddie Muller
Evan Johnson
Fred and Margaret Dunsmore
Noah Cowan
Laura Michalchyshyn
Steve Gravestock
Piers Handling
Stefanie Schulte Strathaus
Christoph Terhechte
Chris Stults
Jon Spayde
Michael Lista
Darcy Fehr
Nihad Ademi
Christina Palassio
Rick/Simon
Evan Munday
Melissa Steele
Thora Cooke
David Snidal
Matthew Rankin
Walter Forsberg
Tam Nguyen
Manitoba Legislative Building
University of Manitoba Archives and Special Collections
Manitoba Archives
City of Winnipeg Archives
Winnipeg Tribune Collection
Erin Hershberg
and as always, George Toles.

This book is dedicated to Aunt Lil.

The script and display type are set in Oneleigh, designed in 1998 by Toronto's Nick Shinn. The face is a playful postmodern look at old-style revival letterforms, an alternate-history 1920s typeface, inspired by once-radical faces like Benton and Cleland's Amersterdam Garamont, Goudy's Kennerly and Koch's Antiqua, with idiosyncratic forms and details and considerably more roughage than the majority of today's digital old-style revivals.

The annotations and captions are set in a digital version of Monotype Bell, which was engraved by Richard Austin for the British publisher John Bell and cast by the British Letter Foundry in 1788. The finely tapered and bracketed serif of Bell and Austin's types became an essential feature of 'modern' type designs. D. B. Updike admired these types and had versions cast by Stephenson, Blake and Company. Monotype made these designs available for machine composition.

Printed and bound at the Coach House on bpNichol Lane, April 2009

Edited and designed by Alana Wilcox
Front cover animation by Andy Smetanka
Back cover photo from *My Winnipeg*

My Winnipeg
80 minutes, 2007

Conceived and directed by Guy Maddin
Executive produced by Michael Burns
Produced by Jody Shapiro, Phyllis Laing
Dialogue by George Toles
Cinematography by Jody Shapiro
Edited by John Gurdebeke
Animation by Andy Smetanka
Production design by Réjean Labrie
Art direction by Katharina Stieffenhofer
Costume design by Meg McMillan

Ann Savage as Herdis Maddin
Louis Negin as Mayor Cornish
Amy Stewart as Janet Maddin
Darcy Fehr as Ledgeman
Brendan Cade as Cameron Maddin
Wesley Cade as Ross Maddin
Fred Dunsmore as himself

Produced by Everyday Pictures/Buffalo Gal Pictures
Commissioned by the Documentary Channel

Coach House Books
401 Huron Street on bpNichol Lane
Toronto Ontario M5S 2G5

416 979 2217
800 367 6360

mail@chbooks.com
www.chbooks.com